Refugee & Terror in Europe

Refugee & Terror in Europe

Jyotirmoy Banerjee

Setu Prakashani
Kolkata Delhi
In Association with
School of International Relations
and Strategic Studies
Jadavpur University, Kolkata.

Refugee & Terror
by Jyotirmoy Banerjee

First Edition : December, 2017
Cover Design : Pallavi Keshri

ISBN: 978-81-933898-0-5

Published by:
Archana Das & Subrata Das
on behalf of **Setu Prakashani**
12/A Sankar Ghosh Lane, Kolkata - 700 006
Phone : +91 33 2219 0704, +91 94330 74548
e-mail : setuprakashani@gmail.com
Website : www.setuprakashani.com

Kolkata Outlet:
2, Shyama Charan Dey Street,
Kolkata - 700 073

Delhi Office:
A43, Mahendru Enclave
Gali No. 3, 3rd Floor, G.T. Karnal Road, Azadpur
Delhi - 110 033

Price : Rupees Two Hundred

Setting by:
Cynosure, 26, Jodhpur Garden, Kolkata - 700 045
Printed by:
Imprinta, 143/2B, A.P.C. Road, Kolkata - 700 006

About the Author

Dr. Jyotirmoy Banerjee, former Professor of International Relations (Strategic Studies), Jadavpur University, Kolkata has over four decades of academic exprience, including frequent research and teaching Stints in Germany, Poland and the USA. Besides winning Fulbright, Alexander von Humboldt and and Goethe Institute Fellowships, each several times, he has been recipient of more post-doctoral grants of the Rockefeller, Erasmus Mundus, Inter Nations and UGC research programmes. From Berkeley to Black Forest and Berlin, from Washington to Wroclaw, from Hongkong to Honolulu his academic peregrinations have stretched worldwide.

A jet-set academic, Professor Banerjee's post-doctoral research, teaching and lecturing span the Universities of Calcutta, Burdwan, California-Berkeley, Pennsylvania, Hawaii (Manoa), Massachusetts, Berlin (FU) and Wroclaw in Poland, St. Francis College, Indiana, German Society for Foreign Affairs in Bonn and Berlin, German Foreign Ministry (AA), and the Toenissteiner Kreis in Cologne. The State Department, US National Security Council and the Library of Congress in Washington DC also featured on his itinerary. He has presented papers in national and international seminars, including the World Congress of the American Association of Slavic Studies in Washington DC and in Honolulu. He was interviewed several times by Germany's Deutsche Welle radio station and the Voice of America. Kolkata radio stations and TV channels often invite him to comment on current issues.

Professor Banerjee's wide-ranging academic interests include US, Soviet/Russian, Chinese and South Asian affairs. His special obsession is with German affairs and strategic issues. He pioneered Strategic Studies at Jadavpur University and innovatively reshaped part of his department's curriculum. He also autodidactically developed several edutainment web sites for his students.

Professor Banerjee continues to serve on various academic boards. His books include GDR and Détente, Germany in Search of Identity, Nuclear World, Strategic Studies and Directed Jihad. Besides, he has published a large number of scholarly articles and monographs in India, Europe and the USA. Beyond English, Professor Banerjee is fluent in German and has working knowledge of Russian and Dutch. Occasionally, he bolts out Elvis style rock numbers with his students backing him up.

Foreword

The recent political violence and turmoil in Iraq and Syria forced thousands of people to cross international borders and take refuge in foreign lands. For months the media flashed reports on how desperate groups ventured on long and arduous journeys risking lives, crossing waterways in makeshift arrangements, walking on lands through the countries of Eastern Europe while the attitude of the host states swiftly turned from sympathy to open hostility. Germany, in many ways the leading state of Europe today, largely accommodated a greater share of the refugees amidst fear of an impending culture clash and a general security risk of allowing potential terrorists to sneak in posing as refugees.

An acclaimed professor of Strategic Studies, Dr. Jyotirmoy Banerjee, explains in this short exposition the nature of the present challenges and the patterns of future possibilities. Professor Banerjee had an illustrious career in the Department of International Relations at Jadavpur University where he taught over a period of four decades and his research took him to places as distinguished fellowships were offered to him. In this book, Professor Banerjee summons his experience and insight to analyse the intertwined contradiction of humanitarian concerns for the refugee and the associated apprehension of courting the agents of terror, especially in the contemporary Europe. Choosing Germany as a case study, Banerjee explores this dilemma in a very lucid style.

The School of International Relations and Strategic Studies at Jadavpur University stands for advanced research and debate on issues of international importance and also for disseminating knowledge of international relations among the general public. The School is therefore pleased to be associated with the publication of the research outcome of Professor Banerjee and believes that it will have a much wider readership beyond a confined academic circle. A word of praise is also due to Setu Prakashani for evincing interest in publishing this short but important piece of work.

April 2017

Dr. Anindya Jyoti Majumdar
Professor
Department of International Relations and
Director
School of International Relations
and Strategic Studies
Jadavpur University, Kolkata.

Acknowledgement

I wish to place on record my gratitude to the following institutions and persons for making this research and its publication possible:

Alexander von Humboldt-Stiftung, Bonn: for unfailingly providing support to my decades of scholarly pursuits, including the present research,

Berlin University (FU): for generously providing office, charming accommodation in historic, elegant and leafy Lichterfelde-West and access to its enormous resources,

Prof. Dr. Anindya Jyoti Majumdar, Director, School of International Relations and Strategic Studies, Jadavpur University, Kolkata, for actively enabling this research work see the light of the day,

Prof. Dr. Ulrich Naumann and Herrn Jiri Kende, former and current Library Directors, FU Berlin, respectively, for always obliging – and with a smile,

Dr. Amit R. Das Gupta and Dr. Stephan G. Humer and many other Berliners for much help, academic and otherwise.

My wife, Shyamali, for helping out with proof-reading.

Jotirmoy Banerjee

Prologue

A prologue relates to drama. The current topic is no less.

Germany is known for its penchant for orderliness. From the *Hausfrau 's Putzfimmel* (housewife's mania for cleaning) to huge production activities in factories, in wartime or in peace, Germany's Teutonic discipline, thoroughness and organisation talent evoked admiration of even its wartime enemies. The enormous onrush of refugees there today from war-ravaged Afro-Asia poses a dramatic challenge to the built-in German sense of *Ordnung*.

While other countries of Europe also face a similar challenge, Germany, the leader, bears the brunt. Berlin's official welcome to an avalanche of refugees descending from alien civilisations and culture has split the country into pro- and anti-refugee camps. That is symbolic of the polarisation of European societies, faced as they are with terrorism and swarming aliens in their midst. The union bit of the European Union is at stake. EU states are quarrelling. So are social groups within most. The refugee onrush has caused Britain to opt for Brexit. The consequent xenophobia and rise of the right-wing in Europe continue to unfold a dramatic scenario threatening an apocalyptic disaster.

As Chancellor Merkel observed, German thoroughness must now be modified by flexibility. This study is an attempt to gauge that flexibility. The flip side of the coin is that while facing the challenge of integration, Germany – and some other advanced countries of Europe – also stand to gain, potentially, from the refugee influx. A declining German population needs work force to keep up the high living standards and support the growing number of pensioners. Indeed, several million Turks helped re-build modern Germany from wartime devastation. The country's enormous productive power hungers after skilled labour in face of declining birth rate. The refugees could be the answer, if they could be sufficiently educated, trained and integrated and kept away from terroristic ideology.

I spent a most profitable time in my favourite metropolis, Berlin, in the fall of 2015 to research the refugee crisis. I saw both pro- and anti-refugee Germans—and other Europeans—in action. My wife and I had to keep away from approaching the historic Brandenburg Gate—my favourite spot--in the German capital as uncharacteristic Kolkata-like "cholbe na!"-type demonstrations with black flags were going on against the government. On the other hand, I also saw posters—again reminiscent of the campus scenes in Kolkata— at Berlin University's FU campus most emphatically welcoming refugees. Welcome signs were also on display in other public places. Several well-off elderly Germans, both ladies and gents, expressed heartfelt sympathy with the plight of the refugees in private conversations, some of the ladies being actively engaged to help out through their church. Perhaps some of them remembered their own ordeals at the end of World War II. Unspoken perhaps was also the lurking fear of the wild Oriental 'hordes'—the Asiatic Soviet occupation troops--who let loose a reign of revanchist terror in eastern Germany, including Berlin, as the Red Army thrust into the heart of the Third Reich.

The Alexander von Humboldt-Stiftung and Berlin University (FU) have long stood by my research efforts and forays in Germany. This time, too, they were immeasurably helpful. Among the most remarkable sources I was able to consult was Thilo Sarrazin's highly controversial book (see *Content)* that I was dying to read. It predicts that Germany is committing an existential *nirvana, a* deliberate *hara-kiri* by indulging rapidly multiplying dim-witted immigrants with an alien world outlook! Sarrazin is consciously "politically incorrect", minces no words, and consequently has been branded racist. I hope that the present work helps as a ready-reckoner reference to the Afro-Eurasian drama affecting millions and entire societies that is strangely so under-reported in India. This work records events as of mid-2016.

Kolkata, April 2017 Jyotirmoy Banerjee

Content

Refuge and Terror in Europe
A Case Study of Germany

In a dramatic warning aimed at "potential illegal economic migrants", the President of the European Council, Donald Tusk, stated: "Do not come to Europe. Do not believe the smugglers. Do not risk your lives and your money. It is all for nothing."[1] Around 10,000 people were stuck near Greece's border with Macedonia at Idomeni at the beginning of 2016, with the vast majority barred from travelling north in the hope of reaching Germany and other countries. The European Union has been scrambling to confront a gargantuan humanitarian catastrophe, the largest movement of refugees since the end of the Second World War. Tensions in the EU have been rising because of the disproportionate burden faced by some countries, particularly the countries where the majority of migrants have been arriving: Greece, Italy and Hungary. In fact, the problem was already on the horizon since the Arab Spring of 2010-11. The Syrian civil war also started in March 2011 pitching the country's Sunni majority against the Shia Alawite President Bashar al-Assad's authoritarian rule. Regional and world powers were drawn in.[2] The rise of the Islamic State as a "caliphate" in June 2014 further complicated the situation.[3]

Terminology

It should be clarified at the outset that throughout this essay, Islam is the great religion while 'Islamism'and related terms like

This essay is part of an ongoing research project which was begun at the Berlin University (FU) in fall 2015. The author wishes to acknowledge his graitude to the Alexander Von Humboldt-Stiftung, Germany, for sponsoring the project.

'Islamist'is used to indicate the use of that religion not primarily for religious or spiritual purposes but rather for political end. The terminology used here is based on expert opinion, including that of the *Bundesamt fuer Verfassungsschutz (BfV),*[4] Germany's internal security agency.

Salafism has both broad and narrow connotations. In its original connotation it implies ancestors or predecessors in Arabic and refers to the first three generations of Muslims, including prophet Mohammed and his companions and followers. Salafism, propounded by the Sunni Muslims, stresses the importance of return to 'pure' Islam of the *salaf,* or pious predecessors. Its goal is to unite the Islamic world and establish a caliphate based on Islamic law, or *sharia.* Those who interpret Salafism in its strictest, narrowest sense include radicals preaching violence to achieve their goals. Not all Salafists are violent-prone radicals, but some are.[5] They preach inter alia jihad.

Jihad is another term that is supposed to have several connotations. According to the *BfV*,

> In accordance with the jihadists' self-designation, this term refers to adherents of the global jihad movement as defined by the ideology of al-Qaeda and related groups. Literally, "jihad" means "effort" or "endeavour". Muslim tradition knows both "small jihad" and "major jihad". "Major jihad" is peaceful. It stands for the individual striving for correct religious behaviour towards God and the fellow human beings. "Small jihad" is of a belligerent nature. It involves the violent forms of struggle in defence of Islam or for spreading the dominion of Islam. However, in compliance with al-Qaeda's interpretation, the term "jihad" is used in connection with the armed fight against alleged "unbelievers" and "apostate" regimes.[6]

Hence, while interpretation of jihad may vary, the term is used most frequently in all popular discourse as meaning "small jihad", i.e. in the al Qaida-defined sense of militant conquest of foreign territories and belief systems under the banner of religion.

The Turkey Vortex

Most of the over a million refugees who arrived in the EU in 2015 came via Turkey, which in turn has an unmanageable number of refugees, mostly from Syria, to cope with.[7] The burden already cost it about $10 billion, claims Ankara. The EU's external border force, Frontex, monitors the different routes migrants use and numbers arriving at Europe's borders and put the figure crossing into Europe in 2015 at more than 1,800,000. The bulk of the refugees came from war-torn Syria, Afghanistan and Iraq, the top three refugee generators and in that order. There followed the Balkans (Kosovo, Albania), strife-torn regions of Africa like Somalia and Eritrea, and even Pakistan and Nepal in South Asia. A failed government in Libya on Africa's Mediterranean coast and a seemingly insouciant Turkey provided two major staging areas for the escaping masses to reach Europe. Most arrivals were by sea, to Italy and Greece (and, to a far lesser extent, Spain).[8] Most of those heading for Greece took the relatively short voyage from Turkey to the islands of Kos, Chios, Lesvos and Samos —often in flimsy rubber dinghies or small wooden boats.

Turkey, sharing common borders with turbulent Syria and Iraq to its south, became a transit country on the refugees' northward exodus to Europe. It pursued an apparently unconcerned policy regarding control of the refugee movements along the Aegean coast. Authorities also tended to turn a blind eye to trafficking and to the growing business of forging Syrian passports. Ankara has had its reasons. It is bitterly opposed to the Syrian government of Alawite Bashar al-Assad who rules over a Sunni-majority country but has excluded the latter from his government.[9] The appearance of Russia on the side of Assad's government complicated matters even more. The Syrian civil war was promoted to East-West rivalry reminiscent of the Cold War days.[10]

Besides, the Shia-Sunni conflict in Syria and Iraq is also a major refugee-generating factor. The conflict is exploited by regional rivals Saudi Arabia and Iran. In the words of the Council on Foreign Relations, it is "widening the fissures" in the Persian Gulf countries.[11] Ankara allegedly has quiet deals with the murderous Islamic State (variously called IS, ISIS, ISIL, or Daesh) which is fighting Assad's regime. Though publicly it strikes an anti-IS pose, Turkey supposedly supplies arms to the IS and buys its oil, thereby contributing to the latter's finances. At the same time, the pose seems at least partly genuine. Of the half dozen or more bombings on Turkish soil during mid-2015-March 2016 (which followed a relatively peaceful two years), most have been blamed on IS. In mid-March 2016 Turkish artillery pounded IS positions across the Syrian border. The bombings in February and March 2016, however, were blamed on the PKK, the militant Kurdish Workers 'Party.

Secessionist Kurdish rebels operate in the eastern part of Turkey and bordering western Syria and Iraq. Kurdish terrorists have periodically blast bombs in Turkey, the latest being in Ankara in March 2016. Turkey retaliated by air strikes on Kurdish positions in Syria. Its army had entered Syria and Iraq on earlier occasions, too. So, as a BBC analysis observes, Turkey finds itself in the midst of a hideous vortex of overlapping security crises, struggling to tackle one without exacerbating another. With each bombing, the precariousness of Turkey's situation seems even more acute.[12] Ankara is playing a complicated game of cooperation and aggression with both the IS and the PKK.

Burdened with millions of refugees itself, Turkey just looked the other way as hundreds of thousands of refugees from across the border with Syria fled the conflict there, transited Turkey and headed for Europe in search of safety and better life. The next country of transit was economically weak Greece, with which Turkey has a long-standing rivalry. So, it was quite convenient for President Recep Erdogan's government to do nothing to stop the refugee transit.

In November 2015 the EU and Turkey signed a deal in which Brussels offered to spend Euro 3 billion ($3.3bn). Facing a backlash from anti-immigration populists across Europe, the EU has been desperate to stem the influx. The deal was struck to ease the burden of some of the 2.5 million refugees in Turkey in exchange for help in reducing numbers travelling to Europe. An additional bonus was the assurance to revive Turkey's long-stalled EU membership talks. German Chancellor Angela Merkel played a key role in forging the deal. Hitherto Europe expressed impatience with the continued high number of people making the perilous crossing over the Aegean Sea. Ankara in turn has been unimpressed with the months it was taking Europe to find the money.

Turkey doubled its demand for aid to Euro 6 billion at its two Brussels summits with EU in March 2016 and reiterated other demands too. Under the pact finally concluded on 18 March, Ankara would take back all migrants and refugees, including Syrians, who cross to Greece illegally across the sea. In return, the EU would take in thousands of Syrian refugees directly from Turkey and reward it with more money (six billion Euros, in phases), early visa-free travel for its citizens and faster progress in EU membership talks. German Chancellor Angela Merkel was again the key driving force behind the agreement.[13]

As Marc *Pierini* observed in a Carnegie Endowment study, Turkey cannot just keep sitting on the sidelines and watch the massive social and political destabilization of the Europe it has sought to join.[14] And *The Economist* put it succinctly,

> Ultimately, Europeans must come to terms with two realities. First, they cannot change geography: they need Turkey because it stands between Europe and much of the Eurasian landmass. Second, they cannot seal their borders entirely: the only alternative to chaos is a fair and orderly migration system, which would most benefit Europe and those fleeing war.[15]

Nearly four thousand deaths were estimated to have occurred during the exodus. It should be noted that many of the migrants are not really political asylum-seekers but economic refugees seeking a better life. By fall 2015 the Arab region came to host more than one-third of the world's refugees, with Lebanon and Jordan under significant strain. War forcibly displaced more than 12 million Syrians in the past four years alone.[16]

The West's Syrian Dilemma

A ZDF TV commentary summed up well the cauldron of the Syrian crisis. Here is a summary:

> We support Iraq's government against the IS – we hate the IS. We hate Assad in Syria, we support the fight against him, but then the IS also fights him. We do not like Russia over the Ukraine issue but Russia is fighting the IS, which we like. Russia and Iran support Assad, we do not like it. Our friends, including the Saudis, also do not like it. Saudis support the IS against Assad and Iran with petrodollars, and we do not like it. Even less do we like the uncontrolled refugee invasion of Europe. So we have to please Turkey, otherwise Turkey will not secure our external borders. Hence, some of our friends are our enemies, some enemies are friends, in alliance against the IS, and some of our friends are fighting against our other friends.[17]

The Cascading Effect

The Balkans

This region is a major generator as well as conduit for refugees.

In response to the refugee onrush Slovenia, followed by Macedonia, Serbia and Croatia nearly closed their borders to refugees. This was in turn welcomed by Austria. Some 13,000 migrants were stranded at the Macedonia-Greece border as of beginning March 2016. The French government was reportedly planning to close a purpose-built camp for refugees and migrants outside the French coastal town of Dunkirk. Paris warned that if Britain went for 'Brexit', i.e. exit from the EU, it would go easy on stopping immigrants concentrated in squalid woodland camps, collectively called "the jungle", on its Calais coast from leaving for the British coast across the Channel. Now that the UK has voted for the exit, it will be small wonder if Paris 'unleashes' the refugees pining for migrating across the Channel. It should be noted here that the Brits have been paying France for extra security to keep those undesirable immigrants away and that it is the fear of mass immigration into the British Isles that may have tilted the vote in favour of the divorce from EU.

East Europe

Further east, Poland and Hungary's ruling conservative parties share anti-immigration sentiment. The current government in Warsaw, elected in October 2015, reversed the earlier government's policy of accepting EU quota for refugees. Its Premier, Mrs. Beata Szydlo, declared that Poland refused to take in the extra 4,500 refugees previously agreed upon since the Paris terror attacks had 'changed the situation' on migrants. Hungary's Prime Minister Viktor Orban's political party launched a campaign for signatures against the European Union's quota system intended to redistribute migrants.[18] Orban even alleged a master plot – leftist-liberal – against the sudden surge of refugees. Budapest extended nationwide a state of emergency as it deployed a further 1,500 police and army troops on Serbian border.[19] Hungarian Interior Minister Sandor Pinter said he would send more police and soldiers to patrol the country's southern borders and would make preparations to erect a fence along its border with Romania – if necessary within 10 days. Hungary's success with "triple defence", i.e. a whole package of "border policing", including the fence, the police and troops defending it, and effective law backing them up evoked both jealousy and inspiration. Austria, initially critical of Budapest, was nevertheless inspired and made a u-turn and announced its own plan to build a fence along its border with Slovenia. The latter in its turn agreed to cooperate, even though both belong to the borderless Schengen system.[20] The two states serve as transit countries from the Balkans to the more northern states of Europe.

More than 386,000 migrants passed through Hungary in 2015 before its borders were closed in October that year. An organiser of the Paris attacks "recruited" some migrants from Budapest's main train station, Hungarian officials said. Hence, refugees were suspect. This sounded much like the Polish justification of pursuing an anti-immigrant policy. Earlier, in September, EU ministers had voted by a majority to relocate 160,000 refugees EU-wide, but as of March 2016 the plan would only apply to those who are in Italy and Greece. Hungary in fact challenged the EU plan to distribute refugees among its member states before a court.[21] Other countries such as Albania and Bulgaria are wary of attracting attention as alternative routes for refugees and smugglers alike.[22] Eastern European nations are not used to outsiders unlike Western Europe, which partly explains their emphatic rejection.[23]

On 4 May 2016 a meeting was held in Prague among Poland, the Czech Republic, Hungary and Slovakia with EU's eastern partner countries (Armenia, Azerbaijan, Georgia, Moldavia, Ukraine und Byelorussia). The EU-Turkey deal—brought into play by Berlin—came under withering criticism as did the provisions of allotting refugee quotas for EU states and ease of travel of Turkish citizens to other European states. Poland's Foreign Minister Witold Waszczykowski called it an April [Fool's] joke.[24]

The Scandinavian Peninsula

Border controls have had a cascading effect elsewhere too. At the turn of 2015-16, Norway's rightwing government proposed a package of new measures that it claimed would make Oslo's asylum policies "among Europe's toughest". Scandinavian countries have been competing with each other to shed their reputations as havens for asylum seekers. Initially, this was not the case. "My Europe takes in people fleeing from war, my Europe does not build walls," the Swedish Prime Minister, Stefan Löfven, told crowds in Stockholm on 6 September 2015. But three months and about 80,000 asylum seekers later, his Migration Minister told parliament: "The system cannot cope."[25]

In early January 2016 Danes stepped up controls at German border after Swedish move to impose identity checks on people travelling from Denmark. Just hours after the Swedish checks were introduced, Denmark announced it had stepped up border controls on its southern boundary with Germany. The Swedish passport checks were leaving large numbers of asylum seekers stranded in Denmark. In fact, all these measures led Germany to warn that the passport-free Schengen zone was in danger.[26]

Role of Germany

But public opinion on German Chancellor Angela Merkel's welcome policy towards the refugees has been volatile, from initial hostile outbursts of anti-refugee collective action, through a massive wave of solidarity and support for refugees, to a strong bifurcation of opinions subsequently.[27] Merkel continued to insist on a pan-European solution. She expected the burden of refugees to be shared by all EU states. But as *The Guardian* reported:[28]

> The German chancellor is said to be angry with the governments of eastern and central Europe which are strongly opposed to being forced to take in refugees. She is said to resent that these EU member states are pleading for "solidarity" against the threats posed by Russia and Vladimir Putin while they resist sharing the burdens posed by the refugee crisis.

Sympathy for immigrants in Europe, and Germany, was badly rattled when the second Paris carnage took place on 13 November 2015 and especially by the New Year's Eve vandalism shortly thereafter, including drunken sexual assaults, in Cologne.[29] The latter event outraged European opinion and provided grist not only to right-wing anti-immigrant propaganda but also to serious doubts among hitherto neutral or well-wishing Germans and other Europeans. Already in October Henriette Reker, Duesseldorf's official for refugee affairs, had been stabbed.[30] The anti-refugee sentiment was also partly reflected in the media. *The Times*, London, predicted inevitable counter-reaction that would increase the stress on Frau Merkel and her welcome policy; the Swiss *Neue Zuercher Zeiung*, the Belgian *De Standaard*, the Italian *Il Messagero* and *Jornal da Republica*, Germany's *Die Zeit* and a host of other print and electronic media across the continent struck a similar refrain: while there should be no generalisation about migrants, the seriousness of such offensive acts as that night in Cologne must not be ignored for the sake of 'political correctness'.[31] On 9 January 2016 there followed demonstrations by the anti-immigration Pegida and counter-demonstrations in support of the refugees in the Cologne main railway station area.

A typical scene of resentment against refugees and political authorities is registered by a *Spiegel* report.[32] The weekly "We Are Germany" Sunday demonstration in Plauen, just south of Leipzig, is to provide a stage to everyday citizens, an idea that goes back to the weeks leading up to the collapse of the former East German state. A speaker takes the microphone to say that he does not have anything against foreigners in principle. But please not here in Plauen. "I don't want Plauen to turn into another Berlin-Kreuzberg, where one sees women in headscarves or even burkas," he says. The audience applauds his words. Regarding crime committed by refugees: "They should be immediately deported." The crowd is rapturous. But more of this trend later when we turn to the rise of the right-wing.

Suffice to note here that "[T]he division between traditionally leftist and traditionally rightist attitudes is disappearing," says a study by the Otto Brenner Stiftung. It speaks of a new "cross-front," where traditional left and right are coming together. The Editor-in-Chief of the *Compact* magazine, which is a favourite of right-wingers, Juergen Elsaesser, is an ex-leftist and former teacher but symbolizes this "cross front", or the New Right. His motto: "Antifa [anti-fascist], Pegida, Mahnwache, left and right, march together," he has called out. "You don't have to love each other. But you do have a civil responsibility: that of showing those at the top where the limits are." Political scientist Markus Linden, from the University of Trier, believes that the new protest movement is primarily united in its distrust of societal elites. Politicians, business leaders, media professionals: they are all suspected of having formed a conspiracy against everyday people.[33]

Meanwhile, a Syrian passport was found near the body of one of the killed gunmen in the Paris attacks, which revealed that the passport-holder had travelled to Europe via Greece, the beaten track of the refugees. The slain young ringleader of the multiple attacks, Abdelhamid Abaaoud, was a Belgian citizen who spent time in Syria.[34] Several of the attackers had a Franco-Belgian background. The attacks occurred at a time when sentiment toward Muslims and foreigners in Germany was turning increasingly hostile.[35] Indeed, US Republican Presidential candidate known for his outspokenness, Donald Trump, thundered that Germany was under "massive attack" by the migrants. As a *Spiegel* commentary observed:[36]

> As inexact and unclear as the facts from Cologne may be, they carry a clear message: Difficult days are ahead. And they beg a couple of clear questions: Is Germany really

> sure that it can handle the influx of refugees? And: Does Germany really have the courage and the desire to become the country in Europe with the greatest number of immigrants?

A popular *ZDF* TV programme, hosted by Maybrit Illner, featured the observation that while accommodation has been provided for the asylum-seekers in German villages, towns and cities, there was no plan for integration.[37] This rouses anxiety among the local inhabitants who are suddenly faced with hordes of strangers with different cultures and life-styles.

Cheating by asylum-seekers was also reported. *Der Spiegel,* which is Germany's premier newsmagazine, investigated a case involving an Albanian family, whose asylum application was rejected by the court, and which therefore switched to bribing officials to get false attestations of psychological trauma. That would make them incapable of travelling and would enable them to escape deportation. A serious psychological investigation should take at least 5 hours but in the case of the 3-member Albanian family, it took less than one hour to check all three! Curiously, attestations of psychological illnesses can be issued by any house doctor. A bribed (euro 1,500 plus) attorney briefed an interpreter to advise the attesting doctor what elements to include in his attestation and how (s)he could sidetrack legal hurdles. Plenty of such dubious attestations are appearing before courts. Only in cases of serious doubt regarding an attestation is an expert appointed. The city of Dortmund reported on 18 March 2016 that more psychological trauma cases were being put forward by the asylum-seekers than physical illnesses as excuse not to leave Germany.[38]

Measles, which had died down since 2002, reappeared in epidemic proportions in parts of Germany since 2015, esp. in Berlin, North Rhine-Westphalia and Bavaria. Its rapid spread was partly ascribed to refugees from countries like Bosnia-Herzegovina.[39]

The leader of Germany's *Christian Social Union* (*CSU*, ruling Grand Coalition leader *Christian Democratic Union's* sister party), Horst Seehofer, has been poignantly critical of Chancellor Angela

Merkel's open-door policy while showing respect to the right to seek asylum as guaranteed by the German Constitution. His critique of the "implementation" deficiency of the refugee policy partly stems from the fact that the CSU operates in the southern German state of Bavaria, where Seehofer is the Chief Minister and which has to face the brunt of refugee arrivals.[40] It is also because his party has been losing ground to right-wing groups, such as the *Alternative for Germany (AfD)*. Frau Merkel also faced flak from within her own party, the *Christian Democratic Union*. Germany may be facing "an avalanche" of refugees triggered by "careless" actions, warned the wheelchair-bound veteran politician Wolfgang Schäuble (*CDU*), the country's powerful Finance Minister, in a thinly-veiled criticism of his boss.[41] Interior Minister Thomas de Maizière (*CDU*) also had reservations but his opposition to Syrian refugees bringing in their families was overridden by Merkel. Schäuble, however, supported him. The other big partner of the ruling coalition, the *Social Democratic Party (SPD)*, has also been critical. It, however, was sympathetic to the family-reunion plan. But on October 21 de Maizière had without telling the chancellor reimposed the so-called "Dublin rules" for Syrians. These EU regulations allow a country, such as Germany, to return refugees to the member state in which they first arrived within the Union. The suspension of these rules was the key technical change Frau Merkel had made with her "refugees welcome" announcement in summer 2015.[42]

Across the spectrum of the ruling coalition in Berlin, there is a broad agreement that Europe must share the refugee burden.[43] The countries which face the initial onrush in Europe are Italy and Greece but the destination of most refugees is skewed towards Germany. This is because Germany is the richest country in Europe and on top of that has a welcoming policy. Merkel, however, acting no doubt under considerable pressure, revised her open-border policy since the height of the refugee crisis at the beginning of September 2015, reintroducing border patrols and suspending the Schengen zone's free travel provisions for a limited amount of time as part of a soft clampdown on the stream of refugees. However, migrants have continued to be accepted in

Germany regardless of border reinforcements, as long as they applied for asylum upon arrival in the country.[44]

According to a study, in spring 2013 the main issue facing EU citizens was the economic situation. On average only one in ten Europeans pointed to immigration as an issue facing the EU. In spring 2014, however, the latter concern was on the rise. In spring 2015 immigration became the main concern of Europeans, ahead of the economic situation and unemployment.[45]

Why the Refugee Crisis?

After five years of war the future in Syria looks bleak. The civil war there, currently internationalised, is the single-most important generator of refugees. It is estimated that one of every five refugees globally is a Syrian. While the bulk of Syrians fleeing come directly from their homeland, there are also those who join them from refugee camps in neighbouring Lebanon and Jordan where their life is in a limbo – no permission to work and their freedoms restricted. But other conflicts, such as in Somalia, Eritrea, Iraq and Afghanistan, have displaced millions of Libyans, Sudanese, Somalis, Iraqis, Afghans, Yemenis, and more fleeing conflicts in their own countries.[46] Young men are also leaving to avoid now-mandatory military conscription by the Syrian army and to escape a war of which they want no part. The relative ease hitherto of the route via Turkey and Greece to the Balkans facilitated the refugee movement. The collapse of the central government in Libya opened a new route for economic migrants from Africa. The estimated price of transport also dropped while traffickers have become increasingly more sophisticated.[47] Since other neighbouring states were unwilling to host refugees, the choice of haven narrowed down to stable, prosperous and initially welcoming West Europe and Scandinavia, most of all, Germany.

There is one, potential, silver lining, or so it seems.

Most experts agree that Europe needs immigration to compensate for its deteriorating demographics, to regain growth, and to maintain its welfare systems. The current wave of refugee arrivals may therefore in the longer term be to Europe's benefit. But the problem is that at present the process is utterly chaotic. And the "cascading effect", as seen above, was striking powerful blows at the very foundations of the European Union at the turn of 2016. Starry-eyed political pundits predicted in the 1990s, i.e. following the collapse of the Soviet bloc, that there lay ahead a smooth ride to ever greater integrations like the EU, that national boundaries would melt away, just like Marx had predicted (though in the context of flourishing, instead of perishing, communism!). Francis Fukuyama announced the end of the Cold War as the "the end of history." The EU was the foremost model of that future world of inter-state integration to an unprecedented degree in recorded history, a model other regional organizations like ASEAN and SAARC followed with envy and zeal.

Today, the refugee crisis has caused European borders to appear again. Hungary's razor-wire fence with Serbia and Croatia successfully choked off immigrant figures from flood to trickle, from 10,000 daily to a few dozens in October 2015.[48] As seen above, Vienna followed suit. The Netherlands stepped up spot checks on its borders with Belgium and Germany, while Germany closed its border with Austria. Denmark raised barriers against Germany. It reintroduced border controls in February 2016 fearing a potential influx of UK-bound migrants, amid French plans to evict thousands of people from camps together called 'the Jungle' near Calais. Migrants and refugees arriving at the Belgian town of La Panne, on the border with France, were turned back. Belgium again closed its borders with France following the 22 March 2016 terror attacks, of which more later. UK's Premier David Cameron called for an "emergency brake" on migration within the European Union (EU) as the French Prime Minister warned that Europe would collapse if it accepted every refugee fleeing Syria and Iraq.

As of early 2016 the 28 EU member states have difficulties to agree on an EU-wide effective mechanism. The Dublin Regulation is not working effectively. States in Central and Eastern Europe (Macedonia, Hungary, Poland, Serbia, Croatia, Slovenia) refuse to accept migrants. Germany, Austria, Denmark,

Sweden, France and Belgium have re-imposed border controls. The borderless Schengen system,[49] which was a marvel, has threatened to fall apart.

The UN High Commission for Refugees (UNHCR) despaired over Europe's lack of solidarity in handling the refugee crisis.[50] The element of close cooperation on handling refugees is distinctly missing in most cases. Cooperation has largely been replaced by non-cooperation and even by suspicion and jealousy. The free-and-easy Schengen visa system, which was a model of borderless Europe and allowed free movement within its 26 European member states to everyone, including non-EU citizens, is at stake. The very viability of the EU is under a cloud at this moment. The unity of the Union is in disarray as the latter individually and collectively grapples with the refugee onrush.

Many Europeans fear the influx of masses of foreign people as a threat to their established way of life. Populist movements exploiting these fears are therefore gaining ground in many countries. For these groups, anti-immigration feelings go hand in hand with rejection of the EU, which is blamed for this loss of control.[51] This fear of the loss of one's cultural identity in the age of globalization has been aggravated by the sudden sledgehammer onslaught of mass immigrants. It may be tempting to draw an analogy between what the onslaught of Western culture did to Asia, Africa and Latin America, i.e. the Third World, in the earlier centuries and what the Third World is doing today to Europe. Though circumstances are vastly different, the impact on a healthy cultural self-identity, of what Sociologists call, "in-group", or "we" feeling, as distinct from "out-group ", or "they "feeling, is undeniable.

Jan Techau sums up well:[52]

> Politicians have especially avoided the integration part of the refugee issue. Partly, this has to do with ideology. The political Left has steadily argued against immigration policies because it fears that establishing fixed rules will limit migration. The Right has done the same thing but for

> the exact opposite reason: it fears that systematizing migration will only open the floodgates. This constitutes an informal grand coalition against pragmatic problem solving.

Then there are the emotional identity issues. Few other issues have triggered as many as this one. And few other issues have triggered as determined a reaction to protect the national interest as the massive influx of strangers into the homeland.

Countries with well-developed immigration policies, such as the UK, were better prepared even though it is the fear of immigrants that is said to have caused 'Brexit'. Others, where no tradition of integrating large numbers of foreigners into the mainstream exists, such as the Czech Republic, Hungary, and Romania, balked at the prospect of taking a share of the refugees in.

Identity politics and anti-EU sentiments had already been rife before the refugees arrived at Europe's doorstep. Trying to make the case for the integration of hundreds of thousands of refugees into host societies under today's circumstances is especially hard.

Refugees and Terror

The narrative so far has focused on the immediate socio-economic-political problems that Europe has been facing from the avalanche of refugees. However, an even more acute problem is presented by the certainty that among the hundreds of thousands of genuine asylum-seekers Trojan horse terrorists have been sneaking in. They are only too eager to destroy civilised society from within. As the chief of Russia's Federal Security Service (FSB), Alexandr Bortnikov, observed at an international security conference in St. Petersburg in July 2016, sleeper cells set up by Islamic State, Nusra Front and al-Qaida in Europe were "coming to life as a result of the influx of the militants together with numerous migration flows."[53]

When they are added to the threat posed from indigenous radicalised "invisibles",[54] the disaster, human, material and psychological, looming ahead becomes brutally palpable. The West's dilemma today: with the sure knowledge that the invisible army and the marvellous handiwork of Epeius[55] are lurking, how much liberty, privacy and democracy to preserve versus how much of intrusion to permit into private lives.[56] New York, London, Madrid, Paris, Brussels, Istanbul, Munich. . .who's next??? As the sleek IS online magazine *Dabiq* comments, while many devout followers of the IS caliphate carry out their duty by undertaking the *hijrah*, or migration, to the Islamic State, "others do so by defiantly terrorizing the crusaders in their very strongholds."[57] Videos, probably of IS-origin, which showed Cologne airport and the German Chancellor's office in flames, did little to soothe frayed German nerves.[58]

With the Soviet troop pullout from Afghanistan and the breakup of former Yugoslavia in the 1990s, the first Islamist terrorists entered Europe to fight in the Kosovo crisis.

The permeability of Europe's borders has enabled the Islamic State to carry out spectacular attacks at will. A *New York Times* (*NYT*) analysis provides interesting insights on this:[59]

> In the immediate aftermath of the Paris terror attacks on Nov. 13, French investigators came face to face with the reality that they had missed earlier signs that the Islamic State was building the machinery to mount sustained terrorist strikes in Europe.

The French antiterrorism police compiled a 55-page report in the weeks after the attack, which it presented to France's Interior Ministry.

> The attackers (the NYT went on) sent by the Islamic State's external operations wing, were well versed in a range of terrorism tactics—including making suicide vests and staging coordinated bombings while others led shooting sprees—to hamper the police response, the report shows. They exploited weaknesses in Europe's border controls to slip in and out undetected, and worked with a high-quality forger in Belgium to acquire false documents.

Belgium is also known for relatively easy access to small-arms. There were 18 people in detention in six countries on suspicion of assisting the attackers.

Further,

> French officials have repeatedly warned that more strikes are possible, saying security and intelligence officials cannot track all the Europeans traveling to and from Islamic State strongholds in Syria and Iraq. And Western intelligence officials say their working assumption is that additional Islamic State terrorism networks are already in Europe.

How true!

Within three days of this report a more unpleasant surprise was to come—this time in Brussels. To be sure, at the turn of 2016

Belgium had reportedly succeeded in preventing a terror strike in its capital. But coordinated multiple attacks took place in Brussels on 22 March 2016 despite Belgium having been at its highest alarm level of four around New Year's Eve. Indeed, several European capitals like Brussels, Paris, Berlin, Moscow and London had scaled down their New Year's Eve celebrations and stepped up security measures.[60] The assaults followed the by now familiar pattern of multiple attacks taking place simultaneously. The pattern had manifested itself as early as 26 November 2008 in Mumbai by Pakistan-based Islamist terrorists. The assault had lasted three days. Soon after the gun and bomb assaults in Paris on 13 November 2015 it became clear that several bombers had come from Belgium and that some of the bombs had been made in an apartment in Brussels. In fact Abdelhamid Abaaoud, the Belgian-Moroccan ringleader of the Paris assaults, now dead, reportedly had claimed the migrant crisis made it easy for the jihadists to travel freely across Europe. He posed as a Romanian migrant following the attacks and also reportedly said he had entered Paris with 90 other assailants.[61] On 8 April 2016 the third 'man in the hat' who was shown in CCTV footage as accompanying the two suicide bombers in Brussels' Zaventem – about 12 km (seven miles) northeast of the city – and who had escaped, was tracked down and arrested in Belgium. He turned out to be 31-year old Belgian-Moroccan Mohamed Abrini, an ex-convict. Both he and at least another of the six arrested that day, named just Osama K, had entered the oft-beaten refugee track of Greece from Syria with migrants last year, using fake Syrian passports.[62]

Najim Laachraoui, Khalid and Ibrahim el-Bakraoui, both brothers convicted criminals and suicide bombers in the Brussels attacks, the Abdeslam brothers, Bilal Hadfi, Paris-attacks ringleader Abdelhamid Abaaoud and Chakib Akrouh, and probably some more were connected with both the Paris and Brussels attacks and belonged to the same IS network. Despite denial by German Justice Minister Heiko Maas that there was no connection between the assaults and Germany, the *Spiegel* and the *Welt am Sonntag* newspaper reported otherwise. These publications reported that Abaaoud had at least once visited

Cologne in the past and bought a car, had lived in the north Syrian town of Asas near the Turkish border with some members of the Islamist "Lohberg Brigade" from Dinslaken in the state of North Rhine-Westphalia in early 2014, and that possible links between the assaults and the supply of assault rifles from the German state of Baden-Wuerttemberg to an address in Belgium were under investigation.[63]

The NY Times, quoted above, concludes:

> The attacks suggested that nearly two years of previous, failed attacks overseen by the leader of the Paris assault, Abdelhamid Abaaoud, served as both test runs and initial shots in a new wave of violence the Islamic State leaders have called for in Western Europe and Britain.

On the explosives used, the *NYT* says:

> Peroxide-based explosive, triacetone triperoxide, or TATP, has become the signature explosive for Islamic State operations in Europe.[64] It can be made with common products—hair bleach and nail polish remover—easily found over the counter across Europe."Their ingredients, when combined, are highly unstable and can explode easily if mishandled," Peter Bergen, the director of the National Securities Studies Program at the New America Foundation, said during recent congressional testimony. "To make an effective TATP bomb requires real training, which suggests a relatively skilled bomb-maker was involved in the Paris plot, since the terrorists detonated several bombs. It also suggests that there was some kind of bomb factory that, as yet, appears to be undiscovered, because putting together such bombs requires some kind of dedicated space.

The UK is also worried.

The dreaded IS terror group is exploiting the refugee crisis to smuggle its members into Europe to create sleeper cells, British intelligence agencies have warned. The suspected terrorists are mainly travelling on fake Syrian or Iraqi passports which are now so sophisticated that it is almost impossible to distinguish between genuine refugees and terror suspects, *The Telegraph* (online), UK, reported. Citing security officials, the newspaper said it also meant suspects who were under watch by the intelligence agencies suddenly vanish. "Islamic State is skillfully exploiting the migrant crisis to smuggle terror cells from Syria into major European countries such as the UK," a top intelligence official said. *The Telegraph* further reported that Frans Timmermans, the first President of the European Commission, said that the majority of those coming to the EU are not fleeing war or persecution and that they should be deported. He cited internal figures held by Frontex, the EU border agency.[65]

"Jihadists travel to Raqqa (Syria) to meet up with ISIL commanders, where they receive training and new passports. They then make their way back to Europe posing as migrants with new identities, making it virtually impossible for security officials to detect potential terrorists among those fleeing persecution," the British official said.

The House of Commons Home Affairs Select Committee (HASC) is examining the issue of fake passports being used by suspected terrorists to gain entry into the UK. "It is deeply concerning that the migration crisis may be being used as cover for terrorists seeking to commit violent acts in Europe," Indian-origin lawmaker and Chair of the committee Keith Vaz said."The HASC has heard evidence from the Greek Ambassador, who made it clear that Greece does not have the required technology to identify fake Syrian passports," he said.

"It is vital for our national security that the UK, and EU as a whole, provides resources to secure the external border to prevent future atrocities like the attacks in Paris last year, and ensure international databases are up to date," Vaz said.[66]

U.S. Special Studies on The Refugee-terror Syndrome in Europe

A number of studies have been conducted in recent years in the USA and by the UN on the "'foreign fighter" threat. These include studies by the U.S. Department of Justice, the House of Representatives bipartisan Homeland Security Committee, The Brookings Institution, UN Department of Public Information, etc.[67] As a Council on Foreign Relations report states:[68]

> [Americans] worry about terrorists stealing across the United States' border with Mexico concealed among illegal immigrants. The Pentagon wages war in the Middle East to stop terrorist attacks on the United States. But the growing nightmare of officials at the Department of Homeland Security is passport-carrying, visa-exempt mujahideen coming from the United States' western European allies.

Here we shall take a brief look at two House of Representatives reports dated respectively September and November 2015. These reports present analyses of the Islamist terrorist threat to the West. While their primary concern is US security, they are relevant in terms of their observations on the European security situation. The September report has the following to say:[69]

> Today we are witnessing the largest global convergence of jihadists in history, as individuals from more than 100 countries have migrated to the conflict zone in Syria and Iraq since 2011. . . Over 25,000 foreign fighters have traveled to the battlefield to enlist with Islamist terrorist groups, . . . These fighters pose a serious threat to the United States and its allies. Armed with combat experience and extremist connections, many of them are only a plane-flight away from our shores . . . Of the hundreds of Americans who have sought to travel to the conflict zone in Syria and Iraq, authorities have only interdicted a fraction of them. Several dozen have also managed to make it back into America.

The report further expressed amazement at the unprecedented speed at which Americans are being radicalised by violent extremists. It laments that "gaping security weaknesses oversea – sespecially in Europe – are putting the U.S. homeland in danger by making it easier for aspiring foreign fighters to migrate to terrorist hotspots and for jihadists to return to the West. Despite improvements since 9/11, foreign partners are still sharing information about terrorist suspects in a manner which is ad hoc, intermittent, and often incomplete."

The study made 32 Key Findings and associated recommendations. Of interest to our purpose is the following determination:[70]

> A number of foreign partners have been slow to update their counterterrorism laws to keep pace with the threat, including several key countries in Europe. . . .Unfortunately, the European countries where migrants land are not inclined to thoroughly vet them. Under European law, refugees must be [sic!] stay in the country where they arrive and are registered. . ..Some refugees are screened against counterterrorism databases, but the Task Force was told the majority of arrivals are not. Extremists who blend in with these asylum-seekers and make their way onto the continent could easily obtain European passports within a few short years and have visa-free access to the United States.

The September 2015 report went on to express shock at the European way of handling refugees:[71]

> "Nobody checked us upon reaching Italy," one Syrian migrant named Muhammad reported. "No coast guard, no policeman ever asked if we had papers. Nobody registered us, nobody took a photo of us, nobody took our fingerprints, no one asked us who we were.". . .The refugee quoted above, Muhammed, is now settled in Germany but warns that others could follow his same path to commit acts of terror. "Any IS terrorist could have entered Italy and traveled further into Europe without any problem," he explained. "IS members can take their guns and hand grenades with them, because the Italians even never checked any of the luggage."

A *New York Times* report confirmed the above observation. "We don't share information," said Alain Chouet, a former head of French intelligence. "We even didn't agree on the translations of people's names that are in Arabic or Cyrillic, so if someone comes into Europe through Estonia or Denmark, maybe that's not how we register them in France or Spain."[72] As Wolfgang Bosbach, CDU politician, observed, standardised information exchange was needed among EU states over possible attacks; only

5 of the 28 states, said he, supplied 90 per cent of all data to European data banks. Further, his remarks confirmed Chouet's, that problems of coordination included 28 EU states spelling a suspect's name in different ways, each according to its own language.[73] This surely leads to confusion and delays. The EU could perhaps learn from how multi-lingual India manages similar problems.

Two months later there came another report from the US House. In November 2015 a year-long study by the Majority Staff of the House Homeland Security Committee on security concerns regarding the Syrian refugee crisis was published. The study concluded that the Administration's proposal of "surge" admissions of Syrian refugees into the United States would have a limited impact on alleviating the overall crisis but could have serious ramifications for U.S. homeland security. "Additionally," it went on to note that "widespread security gaps across Europe are increasing the terrorism risk to our allies and present long-term implications for the U.S. homeland."[74] Top-most among its ten findings was: "Finding 1: *Islamist terrorists are determined to infiltrate refugee flows to enter the West—and appear to already have done so in Europe.* At least one terrorist responsible for the Paris attacks is suspected of having entered Europe through refugee flows. *In the days leading up to the Paris attacks, officials in Europe warned that IS was deliberately targeting these routes.*" (Emphases added).

More ominously the study observed:

Warnings have been mounting that IS is focused on deploying operatives to the West, especially Europe. *A French citizen who returned from Syria said the war zone had become "a factory of jihadists trained to hit France and Europe in the very near future,"* according to a report in recent weeks from France's Justice Ministry. (Emphasis added).

This came against the background of multiple attacks in Paris which took place in 2015, on 7 January (the *Charlie Hebdo* attack claimed by the Al Qaeda in Yemen) and again on 13 November. One of the January 2015 Paris attackers shot dead by the police one year later turned out to be the Tunisian Tarek Belgacem. He reportedly had 20 identities, just smoothly sailed through many countries of Europe and lived in Germany as an asylum-seeker.[75]

The Franco-Belgian Angle to Terror

In mid-January 2016 Moroccan police arrested a Belgian of Moroccan descent near Casablanca with direct links to the Islamist gunmen and bombers who carried out the November 13 Paris attacks that killed 130 people. He had travelled from Syria via Turkey, Germany, Belgium and the Netherlands. He had fought in Syria with al-Nusra front before joining the Islamic State. Najim Lachraoui, bomb maker and suicide bomber in the Brussels airport attack, had also visited Syria in February 2013.[76] The Paris and Brussels attacks brought out tiny Belgium's oversized role in the European theater of jihad. Of its 11 million population, Pew estimates put Muslims to about 6 percent as of 2010. But Belgian and French nationals make up around a quarter of the Europeans who went to fight in Iraq in the mid-2000s. The country has provided a steady flow of fighters to IS in the Middle East—including Abdelhamid Abaaoud, the 27-year-old Belgian mastermind of the November 13 attacks in Paris—and has been the site of planning of attacks in Europe.[77]

Both France and Belgium have large numbers of immigrants who are poorer and isolated from the mainstream culture. Both countries have also seen far-right, anti-immigrant parties rise by loudly declaring a Muslim menace. Experts also say it is comparatively easy to acquire illegal guns in Belgium, making it an attractive base for operations. *The Washington Post* notes that Belgium's bilingualism – Flemish and French – makes it hard for immigrants who only speak French to find work and assimilate.[78] And deep distrust between French- and Flemish-speaking government officials has created an elaborate and sclerotic security apparatus that does not always deal with threats efficiently and promptly.

In particular, Belgian jihadism is concentrated in Molenbeek.[79] It's a neighborhood of nearly 100,000 people in Brussels, northwest of the city center, which has had a large Muslim population for many years. It is just a stone's throw from the heart of the European Union, but this densely populated district of Brussels has 40% youth unemployment. Deprivation, petty crime and radicalisation go hand in hand with drinking, smoking cannabis and fighting. This is combined with resentment towards white Belgian society for its perceived discrimination against Arabs. No wonder such an environment generates young jihadis as fighters in Syria, and as terrorists in Europe. As *The Daily Star*, UK, observed, "Whether it be the 2004 Madrid train bombings, the Brussels Jewish museum massacre in 2014 and the following year a foiled shooting spree on a high-speed Amsterdam-Paris train, it is all connected to Molenbeek in some way or other. More recently, jihadis also launched the sickening November 2015 Paris attacks and the Brussels killings in March 2016."[80]

There are 22 known mosques in the district. Molenbeek shares some characteristics with the banlieues (suburbs) in France—densely populated, large immigrant populations, very high unemployment, complaints of inadequate government services, isolation from the central city and corridors of power. The central figure in Belgian militant Islamism was Fouad Belkacem, a 33-year-old preacher of Moroccan-descent and founder of the group Sharia4Belgium, a major feeder for fighters in Syria and Iraq. He is serving a 12-year prison sentence.[81]

There are many gaps in the European methods of immigration control and registration which enable miscreants to abuse those systems. Privacy concerns, bureaucracy and reluctance to share police powers and information make swiftness and efficiency difficult. Hence, sometimes early enough warnings, e.g. from US intelligence, have not been acted upon.

On 18 March Salah Abdeslam, the only surviving attacker of 13 November Paris attacks, was wounded in a gun fight with the police and arrested in Molenbeek[82] after a four-month manhunt. Within four days of the arrest, suicide bombings and gunfire took place in Brussels' Zaventem airport in the early morning of 22 March and, about an hour later, at the Maelbeek metro station near EU headquarters. At least 31 people, including the three suicide bombers, were reportedly killed[83] and over 200 wounded. IS claimed responsibility. The timing of the attacks, coming within days of Abdeslam's arrest, seemed like it was in revenge, though their planning might have been on the anvil earlier.[84] CNN's security expert Peter Bergen appeared on TV to report that US intelligence had estimated that about 6,900 Westerners had gone to Syria to join the IS.[85] The latter must have relished the panic it unleashed once again in the West. TV channels reported that not only Brussels was locked down as a result of the assaults, high-level alerts spread quickly all over Europe and even to New York.

As a RAND study observed, "There have been a growing number of attacks and plots across the West tied either formally or informally to Syria and Iraq. These include attacks in Garland, Texas, in May 2015; Copenhagen, Denmark, in February 2015; Paris, France, in January 2015; Sydney, Australia, in December 2014; Ottawa, Canada, in October 2014; and Brussels, Belgium, in May 2014. More broadly, there were over 20 terrorist plots in the West either directed or provoked by extremist groups in Syria between October 2013 and January 2015."[86] This was not counting the spate of follow-up attacks, worldwide (Istanbul, Dhaka, Baghdad), as of this writing (July 2016).

The House Homeland Security study further noted that Syrian refugees were sporadically reporting that they had seen suspected IS fighters in their midst. An international terrorism research organization published a bulletin in September warning that there were already a number of reported cases of IS infiltration of refugee routes. The study further noted that "Recent warning signs have raised concerns that. . .Islamist terrorist groups have been attempting to infiltrate refugee flows." For instance, "in October 2015, Germany was reportedly investigating 10 cases of suspected terrorists posing as Syrian refugees or committing war crimes abroad."[87]

The House study's Finding numbers 2-4 warned that admitting Syrian refugees into the USA would be a risky business in the face of lack of adequate information about them and would overload vetting agencies.

It is worth quoting at length some of the other Findings:[88]

Finding 5: Europe's open borders are a "cause célèbre" for jihadists.

* It is no secret that refugees have found it remarkably easy to enter Europe. Border security along the European Union's frontiers is weak, and Committee staff found that despite calls for tighter controls, some countries were still willing to "look the other way" to allow refugees to enter *en masse* in hopes they would pass through and seek asylum elsewhere.
* EU President Jean-Claude Juncker has warned countries to stop "waving people through" if Europe intends to get the Syrian refugee crisis under control.
* Director of National Intelligence James Clapper recently noted that European security weaknesses could allow IS to widely disperse operatives onto the continent, a fear that has been validated in the wake of the Paris attacks.
* Europe's 26-country Schengen Area is ground zero for the continent's terrorist travel woes. Members of the area have abolished border checkpoints and passport controls to allow anyone inside it to move effortlessly between the many countries. But in addition to helping tourists, the wide-open area has benefited a number of terrorists who have criss-crossed the continent freely while plotting acts of terrorism.

Finding 6:

European governments face substantial obstacles to information-sharing and are stymied by a lack of internal border checks in their efforts to keep track of terrorist suspects.

Foreign officials in Western Europe who spoke with Committee staff said that already some asylum-seekers had been identified as having potential terrorism ties but by the time they were flagged, the individuals had already left the area. Authorities in refugee "transit" countries also expressed the same concerns, as noted below.

* The absence of common European police and intelligence services magnifies the challenges in locating and monitoring such potential extremists. Indeed, extremists are crossing borders more quickly than the information needed to stop them. Individual European states face serious legal and bureaucratic barriers to intelligence information sharing.
* Jihadists are well-aware of the benefits of Europe's permissive travel environment. An IS e-book published this year [2015] advises aspiring fighters about the ease of traveling undetected across the European continent. The now-deceased IS operative known as "Jihadi John" reportedly traveled freely through Europe despite being on a terrorist watchlist. Similarly Hayat Boumeddiene, an associate of the terrorists who attacked Charlie Hebdo and a kosher market in Paris, was known to French police but avoided detection by leaving the country, driving to Spain, and boarding a flight for Turkey. "I had no difficulty getting here," she bragged from Syria in an IS- published interview.
* The assailant behind an attempted terrorist attack in August on a high-speed train from Amsterdam to Paris—Ayoub El Khazzani—reportedly traveled easily between France, Belgium, Austria, and Germany before launching his attack, despite being on several European watchlists.

Finding 7 determines the following:

* Glaring security gaps along refugee routes into Europe—especially lax security screening of travelers—make the pathway highly susceptible to terrorist exploitation. "There are no real controls," one diplomat in the region explained. "[The authorities] take fingerprints, accept whatever identification they provide—if they have one—and send them on their way." A large proportion of the refugees and migrants that entered Europe in 2015 were unregistered, and even those

who were registered upon arrival went through a process that was rife with security holes, the Committee's review found.

* Fraud has been widespread. Refugees and economic migrants were able to provide false documents, names, nationalities, and other information to authorities who had limited means to cross-check and validate the information, given the volume of travellers and finite police resources. While the overwhelming majority of these travellers were unlikely to have nefarious intent, the security gaps have been a boon for extremists and returning foreign fighters, some of whom may have been on terrorist watchlists but would likely not be detected due to deficient screening.
* Border police in one country visited by Committee staff explained that they did check some individuals who seemed suspicious against criminal and counterterrorism databases; however, they admitted that such individuals are usually gone by the time authorities receive information back on them.

Finding 8 states that the Mediterranean and Balkan countries were becoming a new "terrorist turnpike" into the West due to particularly poor information sharing and weak vetting systems. As of early 2016 rather than stopping the flows, some of these countries were accelerating the travel of refugees toward their final destinations in places like Germany and Sweden and even providing means of transport. This made it easier for potential extremists to make their way into the continent undetected. One refugee interviewed by Committee staff expressed amazement at how quickly his travel into Europe was being facilitated–aided by ease of access to ferries, a steady stream of buses, and free train rides sponsored by governments eager to move the refugees away from their territory. These European border states are in many cases the least equipped to conduct comprehensive security screening and vetting of travellers. The attackers in Paris appear to have moved easily between Belgium and France and in some cases between the Middle East and Europe.[89] A "pass-the-buck" mentality permeated the region, with a number of transit countries arguing that it was the responsibility of the previous country to do thorough security screening and vetting of refugees.

Finding 9 observes that Syrian refugee populations in Europe have already been directly targeted by extremists for recruitment, and in the long run certain communities in which they resettle were likely to become "fertile soil" for violent radicalisation. Over the long term, government leaders across Europe were worried that these populations would fail to be integrated into society and would maintain close ties to the world's most volatile terrorist safe haven, increasing the odds of potential radicalisation. Many European countries lacked the resources to establish effective assimilation programmes, and even when they did, officials and non-governmental organizations expressed concern that they often lost track of these individuals once they declared asylum because of the ease of movement between European countries.

Finally, **Finding 10** reaches a most damaging conclusion on the European handling of refugees. It submits that "America's security is put at risk *when partner countries fail to conduct adequate counterterrorism checks on refugees and are unable to cope with the radicalisation challenges created by mass migration!*"[90] (Italics added).

This is confirmed by Turkish President Erdogan who accused the Belgian authorities on 24 March 2016 of being soft on militant groups and said they should account for intelligence failures in the run-up to Islamic State suicide bombings in Brussels. He said European authorities had shown themselves "incapable" after Turkey deported Brahim Abdeslam, one of the Brussels attackers, in July 2015. He was subsequently released in Belgium. Similarly, the FBI had warned Dutch police about two of the Brussels attackers one week before they blew themselves up, *Reuters* reported.[91] Bungling was also evident in that Belgian police failed to inform their French counterparts last year that Salah Abdeslam was a suspect in the November Paris attacks. So while Abdeslam was stopped by French police as he fled to cross the Belgian border, he was not detained.[92]

Yet another case of incompetence related to the el-Bakraoui brothers (Khalid and Brahim), who suicide-bombed the Brussels airport and the Maelbeek subway. One of them had been a convicted armed robber who violated prison release conditions. But he was never pursued.[93] In the wake of the attacks a string of failures by security services has come to light, including poor communication between security agencies in different European countries. When the Brussels airport partially reopened on 3 April 2016, the police in an unusual move alleged in an open letter to the media that 50 IS supporters were still working at the airport.[94] "No need to fool ourselves. What we have in front of us is a complete failure," a French government official told *The Wall Street Journal*.[95]

Of the seven recommendations that followed in the House study, the very first stated:[96]

> Immediate action must be taken to temporarily suspend the admission of Syrian refugees into the United States until the nation's leading intelligence and law enforcement agencies can certify the refugee screening process is adequate to detect individuals with terrorist ties.

This recommendation almost sounds like Presidential candidate Donald Trump's warning against admitting Muslim migrants into the USA. It would seem that Trump was merely stating in his campaign what these government reports had already stated vividly.

The US itself was hardly immune from terrorist attack after 9/11 though the threat was not as acute as in Europe. This was due to geographical remoteness from the Middle East hot bed, better and more stringent surveillance methods and technologies, and other factors. On 2 December 2015, a shootout took place in San Berhardino, California. Syed Rizwan Farook and Tashfeen Malik, the radicalised husband-and-wife duo who killed 14 people earlier that day and wounded 22 more, met their end in a torrent of police gunfire. Farook had travelled to Saudi Arabia and had returned with a new, but already radicalised, wife he had met online. In fact, according to the FBI, he and a friend had also entered the radical path "for some time". A Health Department official for five years in California, Farook and his wife talked about martyrdom and jihad as early as 2013.[97] The IS magazine *Dabiq* declared triumphantly that when they were killed, they "thereby attained shahādah in the path of Allah. We consider them so, and Allah is their judge." Chillingly the commentary adds: "Thus, the Khilāfah's call for the Muslims to strike the crusaders in their own lands was answered once more, but on this particular occasion the attack was unique. The mujāhid involved did not suffice with embarking upon the noble path of jihād alone. Rather, he conducted the operation together with his wife, with the two thereby aiding one another in righteousness and taqwā."[98]

The U.S. refugee resettlement programme came under intense scrutiny after it was revealed that one of the attackers in the Paris attack of 13 November 2015 might have entered Europe by posing as a refugee. Since then, more than half of U.S. governors refused to accept new Syrian refugees, and the Speaker of the House of Representatives, Paul Ryan, called for a pause in the programme. CIA Director John Brennan warned within a week of that attack that while accepting refugees from Syria security safeguards to keep terrorists from exploiting the resettlement programme had to be maintained.[99]

The RAND study, cited earlier, maintains that "of particular concern for the United States is the growing number of extremists—both Sunni and Shi'a—that have traveled to (and from) Syria and Iraq to fight. The Syrian-Iraqi battlefield likely has the largest concentration of foreign extremists of any jihadist battlefield in the modern era. There have been over 20,000 foreign fighters who have traveled to Syria to fight".[100]

The Rise of The Right-wing in Europe & Germany[101]

"Angry white men are increasingly backing populist candidates in Europe and the US", noted *The Guardian*. *Der Spiegel* observed: "Even as an image of a Germany taking great pains to welcome hundreds of thousands of refugees has bolstered the country's image abroad, it has also been accompanied by a wave of hatred that cannot be played down. At the center of this second, disturbing narrative is Patriots against the Islamization of the

West, or Pegida, a xenophobic grassroots movement that has manifested itself with demonstrations each Monday mostly in Dresden in the east, but also in other parts of Germany."[102]

The *Compact* magazine in its issue 4/2016 portrayed the German Chancellor wearing a Turkish fez cap on the cover entitled "Merkel im Erdowahn"—an ironic twist on Turkish President Erdogan's name. The discussion was critical of the German Chancellor for making a deal with the dictatorial Turkish leader on continuing the refugee inflow into Europe and Germany. One of the discussants sarcastically observed that Frau Merkel's policy that a pan-European solution to the refugee crisis must be found saw its fruitition in that the Balkan states closed their borders while other European states were making their own arrangements. Chief Editor Juergen Elsaesser, of whom more later, maintained that it was Budapest which was doing the job of Brussels, the European Union capital, viz. securing the external borders of EU by not only securing its own borders but lending a helping hand to Macedonia and Bulgaria to do the same, thereby securing the Balkan flank of Europe from refugee invasion.[103]

Support for the rightwing anti-immigration party Alternative for Germany (AfD) hit a record 13%, according to a poll by *Insa* for newspaper *Bild*, thereby putting it on the pedestal of the third most popular political party in Germany. This despite a split in its leadership. Further north, the popularity of the Sweden Democrats continued to increase since they won a record 49 of the *Riksdag*'s 349 seats in 2014. The Swedish party hit 20% in several polls, on a par with the country's two main political forces, the Social Democrats and the Moderate party.[104] In France the far-right anti-immigration Front National (FN), led by Marine Le Pen, made impressive electoral gains despite failing to ultimately win in the local elections in December 2014. She gained notoriety by comparing Muslims with the Nazis in 2010 at a party rally in Lyon.[105]

Already by mid-2015 the Danish People's Party's (DPP) success in the election was in continuation of a trend of rising support for rightwing parties across Finland, Denmark, Sweden and Norway. The number of asylum seekers had increased noticeably in Sweden and Denmark, particularly since 2013. DPP leader Kristian Thulesen Dahl rode the crest of popularity and called for a crackdown on border, on a so called "welfare tourism" as well as for a hardening of policies towards asylum seekers. The DPP won the biggest vote share in its 20-year history and emerged as the largest party in the bloc of those to the right of the political spectrum. The Danish election continued a trend that began in Norway's 2013 election: the rise of rightwing, anti-immigration parties in Nordic countries.[106]

Over the past two decades, the DPP, the Sweden Democrats, the Finns party (PS) in Finland and Norway's Progress Party enjoyed an upward trend in the elections.[107] Also significant is the fact that attitudes to immigration became significantly more negative in Sweden and Denmark. According to the *Eurobarometer*, a record number of people now see immigration as one of the two most important issues facing these countries. While support for the Finns and the Progress Party dropped slightly in the Finnish and Norwegian elections in 2015 compared with previous ones, both became parties of government for the first time following their 2015 and 2013 elections. While the UK's Independent Party (UKIP) was left almost seatless in the British voting system like first-past-the-post, the fact remains that support for UKIP is comparable with the support anti-immigration parties have in other countries.[108] As *Der Spiegel* observed:[109]

> Running on nationalist and often racist platforms, far right parties have gone from the streets into government, enjoying renewed popularity on local and national levels throughout Europe. In eastern Germany, the far-right NPD party has a foothold at state and local levels.

Governments in Poland and Hungary did not mince their words while making pronouncements on the refugees seeking shelter in Europe. Poland's Foreign Minister Witold Waszczykowski went on record in November 2015 to state that Europe should help the refugees 'liberate' their homeland and, to that end, Syrian refugees should be trained into an army to fight the Islamic State.

Hungarian Prime Minister Viktor Orban declared that his country did not want more Muslims even as refugees were forced off train headed towards Austria and taken to refugee camp. "I think we have a right to decide that we do not want a large number of Muslim people in our country," Orban told journalists outside the EU headquarters at Brussels."We do not like the consequences," he said, referring to the country's 150-year history of Ottoman rule during the 16th and 17th centuries. He was defending Budapest's decision to erect a fence along its border.[110]

At the risk of being politically incorrect, Orban then let the cat out of the bag:

> We Hungarians are full of fear, people in Europe are full of fear because they see that the European leaders, among them the prime ministers, are not able to control the situation.

The PRO Network

PRO NRW (NRW stands for the state of North Rhine- Westphalia) grew out of the *Buergerbewegung PRO Koeln* (simply called *PRO Koeln*) as a right-wing citizens' movement. So did the *Pro Deutschland*, or *Pro Germany* party based in Berlin. An offshoot of the pro-Nazi *German League for Nation and Homeland, PRO Koeln* was founded in 1996. The *PRO NRW* party is led by Manfred Rouhs and Markus Beisicht. In 2004 and won several seats in the city council. Its main platform was protest against the plan to construct a large mosque in the city of Cologne. It was Germany's first anti-Islamic party.[111]

The Alternative for Germany (AfD) Party

The AfD, formed in as late as April 2013 with the initial objective of opposing Germany's European Union membership, has since fall 2015 built up a spectacular populist momentum comparable only to that of the Donald Trump campaign in the USA. As of April 2016 it held parliamentary seats in eight of the country's 16 federal states.

Frauke Petry, leader of the right-wing Alternative for Germany (AfD) party who hails from the state of Saxony that borders the Czech Republic and Poland, said in an interview with the *Mannheimer Morgen* newspaper that border guards "must prevent illegal border crossings and even use firearms if necessary."[112] This generated an outrage among the liberal media and other political parties and even a particularly uncomfortable interview with BBC's veteran Tim Sebastian in his inquisitorial 'Hard Talk' programme.[113] AfD-Vice-President Alexander Gauland observed on a subsequent occasion that it was wrong to permit more refugees with an alien culture to enter Germany. As it was, even many of those Muslim immigrants who were long settled there were not yet integrated. The problem was not with their faith but with the tendency to become politically dominant.[114]

In March 2016 reports circulated that the AfD, while working on its first party programme, was considering to uphold a ban on circumcision that would affect not only Muslims but also Jews. Frauke Petry did not want to go that far, however.[115]

During 30 April-1 May 2016 the programme was adopted in Stuttgart. A major theme in it was that "Islam does not belong to Germany." An attempt to dilute that sentence with "political Islam" failed. Islam scholar Hans-Thomas Tillschneider, who teaches in Bayreuth and is also a spokeman of the right-wing Patriotic Platform, declared that it was neither desirable nor possible to reform Islam to fit in Europe. So AfD is pitted against erection of minarets and muezzin's cry calling for prayers in Germany. Further, the Islamic as well as Jewish method of making halal and kosher meat, respectively, would have to change; AfD demands that the long-standing general law to stun any animal prior to slaughter (to minimise cruelty) be extended also to orthodox Muslim or Jewish religious practice.[116] Further, AfD does not mince its words in its programme. "Multi-culturalism" (*Multi-Kulti*) has failed, it declares. What is urgently needed is integration and assimilation. Those seeking to make Germany their home must show willingness to learn the German language well, both spoken and written, and to adjust to that country's culture, legal and social order and not the other way round.

Meanwhile, as 2015 was drawing to a close, *Der Spiegel* noted that,

> It is still just a radical minority that is responsible for much of the xenophobia and violence. The tens of thousands of volunteers who offer their assistance in refugee shelters every day still predominate. But at the same time, a new right-wing movement is growing—and it is much more adroit and, to many, appealing than any of its predecessors.[117]

The *Spiegel* analysis of the rise of the new right-wing is worth quoting at some length for the insights it provides on today's Europe and especially Germany:

> In the past, the right wing was characterized primarily by thugs with shaved heads, bomber jackets and jackboots—people who had difficulty getting the words "Blood & Honour" tattooed on their arms without a spelling mistake. After the 1990s, the jackboot crowd was replaced by the "Autonomous Nationalists," right-wing extremists who disguised themselves by wearing left-wing clothing, but who were just as violent as their forebears.
>
> These street-extremists are still around, but they have received reinforcements. The New Right comes out of the bourgeois center of society and includes intellectuals with conservative values, devout Christians and those angry at the political class . . . The state and its organs, such as the government and parliament, have become the object of a kind of derision not seen since the founding of postwar Germany. Once again, political representatives are being denounced as "traitors to their people," the parliament as a "chatter chamber" and mainstream newspapers as "systemically conformist." All are insults that have origins in Germany's dark past . . . They were all demonstrations of angry citizens who felt their politicians were failing them . . .
>
> The 1 million refugees who have arrived in Germany in 2015 are now acting as a catalyst for this new right-wing movement. The fear of foreigners, of being "swamped" by them, is bonding the New Right together and drawing more "concerned citizens" into their ranks every day.

The analysis concludes:

> German society seems more unsettled than it has in a long time. In a survey performed by TNS Forschung for SPIEGEL . . ., 84 percent of respondents said that the large number of refugees currently coming to Germany will result in "lasting changes" to the country. Some 54 percent said they are concerned that the danger of terrorism is higher due to the influx of refugees and 51 percent believe that the crime rate will rise. Forty-three percent are worried that unemployment will increase. The answers reflect a deep unease in our society. Many people seem to have lost their orientation. They feel that their concerns are not being taken seriously enough by the federal government, which hasn't exactly given the impression that it has the refugee crisis under control. That doesn't mean that these people will succumb to the siren song of the far-right, but it does mean they have become more susceptible to it.

Two Schools

It is not the purpose of the current exposition to give an exhaustive account of the rise of the right-wing in Europe or Germany. Rather, the narrative that follows is an attempt to give a quick introduction to the growing spectrum of the anti-immigration right with special emphasis on Germany.

The onrush of refugees from predominantly Islamic countries of Asia and Africa has played into the prevalent opinions on the role of Islamic migrants in Europe.

There are basically two types of opinions in Europe regarding that role and its relationship with terrorism. The hitherto prevalent mainstream opinion, officially sanctioned, has been that Islam as a religion is harmless and that the majority of the Muslims living in Europe are peaceful and law-abiding. According to this school of thought, it is just a minor fraction of those Euro-Muslims who are Salafists or Islamists with an uncompromising agenda to follow and ultimately impose the *sharia* (Islamic religious law) in the host societies.

The other, hitherto minority opinion maintains that the religion itself contains a built-in mechanism that will stop at nothing short of introducing a radical change in the culture and values of the host nations in accordance with its own version of the divine truth.

The refugee crisis and the consequent rise of the right on the one hand and the second school of thought are currently feeding each other. Here, we take a look at some of the most prominent advocates of the second school.

Opinions: The Rise of The Right Wing

Geert Wilders[118]

He is one of the 150 Dutch Members of Parliament who, however, is different. He lives with a bodyguard escort and lives in a number of safe houses to escape the wrath of terrorist attacks. But Geert Wilders remains outspokenly against Islam as a religious ideology and may be compared to India's Member of Parliament Dr. Subramanian Swamy in this respect. It is ironic, he says, that he is forced to live like a fugitive in his own country for speaking out against what he perceives as the enemies of the West. He is the leader of the third largest Dutch party, the Party for Freedom or PVV. He produced a film called *Fitna* and wrote the book, *Marked for Death,* both designed to show the purported evils of the religion he opposes.

In Wilders' view, the conflict is civilizational in scope and is being fought on two primary fronts: Europe and America. This immediately brings to mind Samuel P. Huntington's classic, *The Clash of Civilizations.*[119] Western societies guarantee their citizens something that no other civilizations grant them: privacy. As he sees it, "It's one of those things you tend to take for granted unless you lose it. The importance of privacy is unique to Western society with its notion of the sovereign individual. The Islamisation of the West is being aided and abetted by multiculturalists in Europe and America who are enforcing politically correct curbs on free speech designed to silence all criticism of Islam... Islamic societies—including Islamic enclaves in the West—exert tight social control that is indicative of the totalitarian character of Islam."[120]

The Prophet and his followers' *hijra*, or migration, in 622 A.D. to *Yathrib* turned out to be fatal to the latter, maintains Wilders. Taking advantage of its welcome and tolerance, Muhammad proceeded to overthrow the city from within. What was Yathrib became Medina. There, the first mosque was established which became Muhammad's "propaganda center, the headquarters of his state . . . and the barracks of his jihad." For Wilders, Yathrib is the model for the offensive via immigration, or "migration," that Islam has undertaken against the West almost 1,400 years later. The Dutch MP also points to Medina's first mosque as the "prototype" for mosques throughout the West, "primarily a political institution, not a place of worship."[121]

Does the refuge and terror problem today in Europe fit this model?

In the BBC's *Hardtalk* interview, Wilders cites Winston Churchill's book, *The River of War* (1899) to confront his British interviewer. He quotes Churchill as remarking in that book that "Mohammedanism" was "militant" faith and that "we may lose our civilization in Europe." Wilders then proceeds to observe that today European leaders are not behaving like Churchill [opposing Nazi totalitarianism] but like Chamberlain [appeasement].

As the reviewer, Ray Hartwell of *The Washington Times* puts it, for the millions of tolerant citizens of the West, Wilders' message can be captured by paraphrasing what Pericles said to the Athenians about politics: You may not be interested in that ideology, but that ideology is interested in you. So pay attention.

Marine Le Pen

Marin Le Pen is the President of the National Front, a national-conservative political party in France and one of the main political forces." She has spun gold from voter exasperation. . .", noted *Time* magazine.[122] A lawyer by profession, she is the youngest daughter of longtime FN leader Jean-Marie Le Pen. She went on record in December 2010 voicing opposition to Muslim prayer-meetings in public squares. She advocates abolition of the law enabling the regularization of the illegal immigrants. In addition, she strongly favours stopping the policy since 2000 of granting free medical care to illegal immigrants.[123] Le Pen also seeks to establish a moratorium on legal immigration. When the November 2015 attacks in Paris took place, she called for an 'immediate halt' to the intake of migrants into France and demanded a crackdown on Islamists in the country.[124]

In December 2015 the northern French port of Calais became the most right-wing town in France. Firebrand Le Pen's anti-immigration National Front party scored a massive 49 per cent of the votes in the town that is home to 6,000 migrants, all hoping to sneak into Britain. Their vote has more than doubled since the last regional elections in 2010, when there were only around 800 migrants in the town. Calais finds itself overrun with refugees living 'the Jungle', seen earlier, near the port. The Middle Eastern origins of many Calais refugees play into stereotypes. Le Pen's victory was also boosted by fears over the Islamic State terror attacks that killed 130 people in Paris on November 13.[125]

Le Pen, however, has also been careful to soften her stance in order to refurbish the image of her party as racist and ultra-radical and make it more palatable to the French voter.

Viktor Orban

The refugees entering Europe, observed the hardline Hungarian Prime Minister Viktor Orban, look "like an army". In October 2015 he told a gathering of conservative parties from across the continent in Madrid, the European People's party congress, "What he [*sic!*] have been facing is not a refugee crisis. This is a migratory movement composed of economic migrants, refugees and also foreign fighters. This is an uncontrolled and unregulated process. . .Right to human dignity and security are basic rights. But neither the German nor the Hungarian way of life is a basic right of all people on the Earth." Hungary has responded to the crisis by building a steel fence along its borders with Serbia and Croatia.

"Does it comply with the freedom of information and speech that media usually show women and children while 70% of the migrants are young men and they look like an army? Just because we do not consider them as enemies we must not act againt [*sic*!] ourselves. Our moral responsibility is to give back these people to their homes and countries," Orban said. His government later offered to help return migrants who had been refused asylum in fellow EU countries to Turkey.[126]

In a Swiss newspaper interview next month, Orban talked about freedom of speech and expression in Europe. He was critical. He claimed that the "the free and sincere exchange of opinions is less and less a part of the culture of the European political elite." He alleged that "what dominates European public speech today is simply European liberal chatter about nice but secondary topics of lesser significance".[127]

Pegida, the *Politically Incorrect*, and others

Lutz Bachmann, born 1973, is the founder of the far-right anti-Islam group Pegida based in Dresden. On Oct.10, 2014. Bachmann, who has a small photography studio in the town of Kesselsdorf near Dresden, posted a video on *YouTube*. Next day he founded a *Facebook* group called *The Patriotic Europeans Against the Islamisation of the West* (*Patriotische Europaer gegen die Islamisierung des Westens*). Thus *Pegida* was born. They regularly meet to talk about the group's agenda and prepare the weekly marches, held every Monday evening. They also maintain contact with other protest groups across the country. A *Facebook* post summed up *Pegida's* stand quite clearly: ". . .let us take to the streets and show our region that WE ARE THE PEOPLE and that we are tired of paternalism, political correctness, Islamization and the constant insulting of us as Nazis just because we stand up for our country and for Europe!" "We are the people" was the legendary rallying cry of protesters in East Germany in the months leading up to the fall of communism in the country.[128] Other *Facebook* comments reflect the unspoken resentment of many Germans and other Europeans: "What should we do with the 90% uneducated hordes that milk welfare here and bleed our social state dry?" Siegfried Daebritz of *Pegida* remarked in another *Facebook* entry: "We want to gather to oppose the advancing Islamization of our country. We don't want terrorist, Islamist powers to fight their religious war on our streets [Kurdish *PKK* and their Muslim opponents sometimes fall out in public in Germany]. We are against IS, PKK, al-Qaida and all the others".

The Chief Editor of the *Compact* magazine, **Juergen Elsaesser**, whom we have already met, is of the opinion that "Pegida is a grassroots movement. . .It's perhaps the last chance we have left to save our people."[129] He has been a consistent critic of what he calls US "imperialism" and calls for "resistance against the international financial capital and its warmongers in Washington, London and Jerusalem."[130] This sounds like the old-world Marxist-Leninist theory of imperialism controlling international finance as well as the theory of conspiracy by the international Jewry that was an old German favourite from the end of the First World War to the end of the Third Reich. Elsaesser in his blog had even called on the Bundeswehr, Germany's armed forces, to occupy stations along the German borders in order to stop the flow of refugees. "Don't wait for orders from above", he exhorted them. A fall issue of his magazine also featured Chancellor Merkel on its cover with the headline, "The Queen of the People-smugglers."

The German blog *Politically Incorrect (PI)* was founded in 2004, the year the Dutch film director and Islam critic Theo van Gogh was murdered. A right-wing network has come into being with the *Politically Incorrect* members tying up with like-minded groups like the *Buergerbewegung Pax Europa* (the Pax Europa Citizens' Movement), *the German Defence League, PRO NRW* (in the industrial North Rhine-Westfalia region) and the *Buergerbewegung Pro Deutschland* (Pro-Germany Citizens' Movement). Together, they are pushing their political agenda from the periphery to the mainstream. *Pegida* plays an important role in this push.

Michael Sturzenberger, a decade ago spokesman for the Christian Social Union (CSU), the conservative Bavarian sister party of Frau Merkel's ruling coalition-dominating Christian Democratic Union (CDU) party, is currently a prominent voice of the *Politically Incorrect,* and since 2012 also the chairman of the far-right extremist party *Die Freiheit* (The Freedom). He is a regular speaker at *Pegida* events. He does not bother to mince words against Islam and compares the *Quran* to Hitler's *Mein Kampf.* He collected signatures opposing the planned construction of an Islamic center in Munich. By 2014 he already held over one hundred anti-Islam rallies.

As *Der Spiegel* observes, "There have been plenty of movements such as Stürzenberger's in Germany in recent years. They generally begin in response to the construction of a mosque: Reluctance turns into resistance, then hate and violence."[131]

Interestingly, there are a few German authors and politicians with Muslim background who are critical of Islamist extremism and even of Islam as a religion itself. Ahmad Mansur, the Palestinian-Israeli psychologist and author of *Generation Allah,* is one of them. Another is Akif Pirinçci, a German writer of Turkish origin. His two books of essays are *Germany Insane* and *The Big Gayification.* He became another Islamophobic name with his contacts with *Pegida* and the *Freedom Party* and his open and vitriolic criticism of both Muslims and the pliant German authorities.[132] Besides, eleven German Members of Parliament of Turkish origin, prominent among whom was the Green Party leader Cem Oezdemir, came under massive threat following the passing of the touchy Armenian Resolution in Germany's *Bundestag* (Lower House of the Paliament) in mid-2016.[133]

Heinz Buschkowsky

Heinz Buschkowsky, for nearly 15 years Mayor of the rough Berlin borough of Neukoelln with widespread social problems, published his book, *Die andere Gesellschaft* (The Other Society) in 2014. The borough is known for its large Turkish, Arab and Kurdish communities and the more recent influx of Romani people, or Gypsies — who traditionally have a dubious reputation in the West — and Sub-Saharan Africans. The title of his book is meant to suggest that German society may be changed by other ethnicities which might impose their own cultures and values on the country. The otherness may be a unique religion-centric society that Germany had not seen before. For example, he says, in the 1960s and 1970s there was no debate on Islam but there is one now that has increasingly assumed importance over the past 25 years. In his opinion, self-proclaimed representatives of that religion are trying to assert domination over the non-religious secular states.[134] The result, concludes Buschkowsky, is that not really "*multi-kulti*", or multi-culturalism, is there in Germany, as propagated by politicians, but a "parallel society" is operating there. His view in this respect is close to Gauland's of the *AfD*, as seen above.

Like Sarrazin, as we shall see later, he is critical of the state acting contrary to fundamental rights in the name of protecting religious freedom. For him, the criteria of gender equality and monopoly power of the state over the use of force are among the major pillars on which a modern society is based. But the Islamic view of these criteria is poles apart. State intervention in cases of domestic violence against women or children is not permitted. He says he had seen many such cases as Mayor involving especially those Muslim families which shirked education. "*Multi-kulti*", advocated for long in Germany, has failed in the absence of proper integration.

Buschkowsky pleads that he is shocked by the state of paralysis displayed by the judiciary and the police in the face of obvious criminal offences. "It is almost like the paralysed rabbit that stares at the snake", says he.[135] "Why are we so weak?" He wonders. "Why aren't we tackling these disturbing elements with determination?" He feels that there are limits to the acceptance of the migrants' way of life. For example, female genital mutilation (FGM) is widespread among communities in Africa and parts of the Middle East. But if FGM is carried out in a modern state by a migrant community, it should never be permissible even under the excuse of cultural or minority freedom.

Islam, says the erstwhile Neukoelln Mayor, believes in the supremacy of the commandments of the Lord Almighty over all man-made laws. It is a complete guide to life that in effect, he feels, is totalitarian. Community values override any individual preferences. It, therefore, directly contradicts the basic tenets of modern – Lockean – democracy where the individual is supreme and enjoys his liberty and freedom to the maximum extent possible. Modern society separates religion from the state and upholds the supremacy of the constitution and secular law. The two diametrically opposite *Weltanschauungen*, or world views, thus collide.[136] His observations recalls to mind Samuel P. Huntington's thesis of civilizational clash mentioned earlier.

Buschkowsky is worried. Though the fundamentalists among the Muslims are relatively few in number, and the majority of Muslims are as peace-loving as anybody else,[137] yet he senses that there may be a certain amount of religiosity of unusual intensity creeping in, e.g. a shift taking place from non-religious immigrant unions to a coalition of religious and conservative organizations, especially among Turkish immigrants.

Buschkowsky's prescription is greater spread of education. Lack of education, he maintains, provides fertile ground for fundamentalism. That in turn hampers integration. The resulting alienation breeds frustration, the feeling of being deprived. This provides a golden opportunity for the messiahs to recruit cannon fodder. He partly blames the tendency of many immigrants to cling on to their identities and not loosen up just enough so as to integrate, to blend in, with the host society. Religion reinforces that tendency while education liberates.

He says he wants to feel at home in his home country and not be alienated by the constant presence of a totally different culture with its life-style from another place and time. He finds immigrant children's educational performance as poor. Indeed, he quotes official reports to determine that 40% of the immigrant children were incapable of qualifying for technical training (2005 report)"a catastrophe in the making". Further, there were five times more dropouts among school children of the migrants and three times more in the final professional examinations than their German counterparts (2014 report). Here he echoes Saarazin, discussed later. So, in his opinion, there is scope for improvement there. Sarrazin would beg to disagree, however, on the liberating role of eductaion.

Also, Buschkowsky feels that a migrant should have at least a 650-word German vocabulary that is equivalent to five per cent of an average German's. However, a Dutch effort in this direction failed. And, to his frustration Buschkowsky notes that the European Court of Justice decided that setting such vocabulary requirement was illegal and that the migrant's family should be allowed to join him in Germany even without such minimal German word power.[138]

Referring to the New Year's Eve assaults on women in Cologne in December 2015 and other reports of similar acts from eight different German states, he states in a *Deutschlandfunk* radio interview that this was to be expected since the vandals hailed from a cultural environment which held a completely different view of women. For them, ladies moving in the streets at night were nothing but pickups.[139]

Thilo Sarrazin

When published in 2010, the very title of his controversial book created a sensation. *Deutschland schafft sich ab,*[140] or *"Germany does itself in"*, neatly summed up the outrageously frank views of the former Berlin Finance Senator, a Social Democrat and former member on the executive board of the *Deutsche Bundesbank* (central bank) who had also served in the government in other capacities. His best-seller earned the opprobrium from the politically correct elite. Like Buschkowsky after him, Sarrazin calls a spade a spade. His latest book, written on the same vein and entitled, *Wishful Europe, currency, education, immigration why politics so often fails,* slams German Chancellor Angela Merkel in particular, accusing her of being distracted by the propaganda of "We can do it!" rather than taking a serious look at the pressing issues of the migrant crisis.[141]

Some of Sarrazin's outspoken theses which are relevant to the discussion here are as follows. He is fed up of being 'politically correct' and wishes to do some plain speaking. Qualitative changes are accompanying the ageing and declining population of Germany. While the ethnic German component of the population with secular outlook, intelligence and skills befitting an advanced industrial society is shrinking, the proportion of migrants is increasing.

Not all migrants are unsuitable for an advanced society like Germany. Indeed, Sarrazin is all praises for immigrants from India, China, Vietnam and the Far East as the most talented. But unfortunately, he observes, they are lost to the attractions of the USA. While migrants from other regions of the EU and Europe are quick to adopt German culture and fertility rates, this is not so with the migrants from the states of former Yugoslavia, Turkey, Africa, the Near and the Middle East. The latter, in his opinion, tend to have low IQs, are resistant to adaptation to the host country's norms and secular values, and have little inclination to work hard and acquire skills, including the host country's language, preferring to receive government doles instead. They are deeply religious and very fertile. The net result is that the organic composition of Germany's population is showing an alarming trend of increase of the bigoted, unskilled, low-IQ population and the corresponding decline of its secular, capable and skilled counterpart. If this trend continued, it will spell disaster for Germany,[142] concludes Sarrazin in his doomsday scenario. Sarrazin backs up his assertions with a liberal dose of statistics.

The controversial author raises the age-old sociological question as to whether it is heredity (or genes) or environment that determines the low-IQ migrants' tendency to remain in the traditional religious groove even though living in a modern society. He seems to believe that the answer lies in the genes though he does not insist on it.

In his view, the problem lies not in the less-educated component of Germany's population increasing. For then, it would be a question of extending education to it. Here Sarrazin parts ways with Buschkowsky. While for the latter spread of education is expected to have a liberating effect on immigrants and their children, for Sarrazin that is not the case. The problem is that while the—read genetically-determined—part with inherited intelligence keeps shrinking, the other part with less inherited intelligence and deep religious convictions continues to increase.[143] Sarrazin seems to imply that no amount of imparting of education will be of help for the less blessed immigrants; they probably would not be capable of absorbing it. His conclusion: if this trend is allowed to continue, the German will disappear from Germany like the Greek did from Asia Minor. The Germans, he predicts, are already "withdrawing from history", as reflected in government statistics.

In his latest book, mentioned above, he holds the view that the migrants are, "from countries with low educational performance," and their "cultural and cognitive profile is similar to that of the Muslim immigrants from these countries of origin, who are already in Europe. It is therefore [to] be assumed that they develop similarly in educational attainment, labour market integration, social benefit terms, crime and vulnerability to fundamentalist ideas. . ..[T]he recovery of the control of our borders, whether the German or the Schengen area, is the question of survival for our civilization and the survival of our society."[144]

Critics call Thilo Sarrazin racist.[145]

The Islamic Community in Germany Prior to the Current Refugee Waves

There were 4,119,000 Muslims in Germany in 2010, constituting 5% of its population of 81.1 million.[146] 45% of them were German citizens. There are about three million Turks in Germany, the largest ethnic minority there.[147] Turkish immigration to Germany began in the 1960s in response to the post-war German labour shortage. While these workers were expected to leave Germany after their work was completed, half of them ended up staying in the country.[148] Their families followed them. There are 30 active Islamic organizations in Germany. Their members jumped from 38,080 in 2011 to 42,550 in 2012.[149] Prominent among these organizations are *Milli Goerues,* the largest group with around 29,000 members, *Hezbollah* (Party of God), the Palestinian *HAMAS* (Islamic Resistance Movement), the *Muslim Brotherhood,* and the *Guelue Movement.*

The picture prior to the refugee deluge of 2013-16 was as follows. After the Turks, the second largest Muslim population was of Bosnian and Herzegovinian origin, followed by Iran, Morocco, and Afghanistan (the largest in Europe, diminished significantly since the fall of the Taliban), Lebanon, Pakistan,

Syria, Tunisia, Algeria, Indonesia and Jordan. Palestinian refugees often entered Germany from third countries. The German Arab population was approximately 290,000 in 2002. Germany also has had the highest number of Kurds in Europe amongst its immigrant population.[150] Interestingly, although India has the second largest Muslim population after Indonesia in the world, their presence is inconspicuous.

Germany hosts (after France) the largest Muslim population among West European states. In West Europe, the Muslim population shot up from 10 million in 1990 to about 17 million in 2010, according to the *Pew Research Centre* of the USA.[151] They migrated from Muslim-majority areas like North Africa, Turkey, and South Asia from the 1960s, taking low-wage jobs. These European Muslims continued their ties with the '*umma*', or world community of Islamic believers, and segregated themselves from the rest of the European society. In this, surely European mental and social barriers also played a part.

Despite Germany's announcement that it would withdraw troops from Afghanistan, the country remained in the crosshairs of Islamist jihadists. Many German army as well as other ISAF/NATO troops were killed in Afghanistan. Over the past few years instability in Syria and Iraq (and Mali in 2012, till French military intervention in January 2013) and the spectacular rise of the Islamic State replaced the Afghanistan-Pakistan region in importance for the jihadists. On January 12, 2016, a suspected ISIS suicide bomber detonated a blast at Sultanahmet Square in Istanbul, Turkey. The attack killed ten tourists, all of them German nationals, and hospitalised nine other Germans. The German Foreign Ministry confirmed that it was the deadliest attack on Germans abroad in more than 13 years.[152]

Germany, like many other Western countries, is worried about a perceptible trend of Islamist radicalisation of youth, whether they come from migrant families or are indigenous converts. For instance, within four days of the massacre in south France there started a series of attacks in Germany. A Tunisian resident of France drove a 19-tonne truck that killed 84 in Nice on 14 July. On 18 July 2016 a 17-year old youth of Afghan origin attacked and severely wounded several train passengers in the Wuerzburg area in the name of religion and revenge against the West's exploitation. The Islamic State publication, *Amaq,* owned up responsibility of the *IS.*[153] Four days later there followed another attack in a busy Munich shopping district killing nine and wounding more. The Bavarian capital's sense of being a safe city was badly shaken as initially a terrorist act was suspected. The attack was carried out by Ali Sonboly, a 18-year German of Iranian descent – this one was billed as a psychiatric case 'running amok'. On 24 July a third and fourth act of violence by refugees followed. The third attack involved a 21-year old Syrian refugee known to authorities for previous acts of violence. He killed a woman in Reutlingen south of Stuttgart with a machete – apparently a jilted revenge case. A fourth assault was carried out by another Syrian asylum-seeker in Ansbach in the name of allegiance to the Islamic State and its leader, the self-proclaimed Caliph Abu Bakr al-Baghdadi. Mohammad Daleel, 27, from Aleppo, had his application to settle in Germany turned down but was allowed to stay. Denied entry into a musical festival, he set off a suicidal blast that injured many. All these assaults within a week took place in southern Germany, three of them in the state of Bavaria, a primary entry point for refugees into Germany.[154] Though not all these assaults could be attributed to jihadist ideology, the fact that these incidents of violence involved immigrants was enough to set Germany – and the rest of Europe – on the edge.

Islamism/Salafism in Germany

Conservative Muslim life-style sometimes causes friction in Western societies. These involve stuff like Muslim women wanting to wear veil covering their face or the *hijab*, or head scarf, at places of work, demand to ban pork-based food products from German schools with Muslim students – even though Germany is famous for sausages, – dominating university halls for prayer and sometimes turning them into informal mosques, demand to segregate boys from girls in co-educational institutions and swimming pools as well as to build minarets in many cities.[155]

However, these are minor irritations compared to the far greater existential threat posed by Islamism/Salafism, boosted by apparent successes of the Islamic State. Germany's *BfV*, in short, the *Verfassungsschutz* or internal security, reported that in 2014 Salafists continued their efforts to attract public attention with events and provocations, for instance with the *LIES!(READ!)* campaign—started in autumn 2011—and the *Shariah* Police. The Salafist association *Die Wahre Religion (DWR*, The True Religion) went on with its LIES! campaign to distribute copies of the *Quran*. In August and September 2014 Salafists, wearing high-visibility vests with the inscription "Shariah Police", patrolled the city centre of Wuppertal (in the state of North Rhine-Westphalia) and handed out flyers which read "Shariah Controlled Zone"—a method of agitation which has been known from the UK since 2010.[156]

With military success the IS had managed to establish itself territorially as a 'caliphate', thus going beyond being a terrorist organisation. That led to euphoria among jihadists also in Europe.

The *Verfassungsschutz* defines Islamism/Salafism as follows:[157]

> Islamism in Germany is no uniform phenomenon. One characteristic feature common to all of its forms is the abuse of the Islam religion for the Islamists' political objectives and purposes. According to Islamist ideology, there is a divine order which society and the state have to subordinate to. This interpretation of Islam contradicts the Free Democratic Basic Order in Germany, especially violating the following democratic principles: the separation of state and religion, the people's sovereignty, gender equality, and religious and sexual self-determination. . .. Salafism is a particularly radical movement of Islamism. Salafists try to practise the Islam of the first three Muslim generations—the so-called "pious forefathers" (as/salaf as/salih) without adjusting it to our times.

While Germany, like several other European nations, was struggling to democratically accommodate its sizeable Muslim community and the incidence of extreme beliefs of a section of them, the growing disturbances in Syria, Iraq and other regions of the Middle East and Africa directly impacted on Europe.

The influx of over a million refugees into Germany in 2015 and still counting in 2016, mostly from Islamic countries, as well as atrocities by some whom the IS has been slipping in as refugees, have hardly been reassuring for German, or other European, nerves. 'Islamism' and 'Islamist', as we saw at the outset, are terms the Germans reserve for Muslim radicals whose aim is to go beyond spiritual matters alone. There is broad agreement on these terms among experts across frontiers. The *Verfassungsschutz* (the German agency for internal security) *Reports* of 2012 and 2013, for instance, reiterate that 'Islamism' entails not only religion but also control over the entire social and political system. Islamists aim at achieving this either by legal or by violent means.[158]

The defining characteristic of Islamism, seen as political use of religion, is its intolerance of others and glorification of violence against all who disagree, including Muslims. Experts in the West flag it as a fascistic, totalitarian and Manichean ideology masquerading as religion.[159] In the name of 'true' religion, the hardliners are killing not merely non-Muslims but many other Muslims as well. The brutal murder of a number of liberal Muslims including bloggers, gays and a professor in Bangladesh, the attack on a popular café in Dhaka, the series of fire-bombings at the airport in Istanbul, and, strangely enough, a *Ramadan* celebration in Baghdad in mid-2016[160] revealed not only indiscriminate killings but also the worldwide reach of the Islamists, with the Islamic State at the forefront. It is also entirely possible, nay probable, that the random bombings of public places, worldwide, did not discriminate true-believers who might have been coincidentally also in the crowds attacked.

Islamist/jihadist groups started to appear in Europe in the 1990s at first in the UK, France and Italy following the Soviet military pullout of Afghanistan. While no major al Qaeda leaders were present in Germany, Mohammed Atta's Hamburg cell there was partly responsible for the 9/11 attacks on the US. Berlin's troop contribution to the Western coalition forces in Afghanistan and other strategic-military ties with the USA brought Germany into jihadist attention. According to a study in 2014, every fifth German was scared of, or hated, Islam.[161]

In Germany Salafism became particularly noticeable since the US-led Iraq war.[162] Since mid-2012 the civil war-type situation in Syria and Iraq and the founding of terror organisations in the region like the IS or the Jabhat al Nusra led to a significant increase in jihad-motivated travel to these countries. The proclamation of the Islamic State Caliphate on 29 June 2014 must have reinforced the factor of travel for fighting jihad. At the same time a significant number of people returned to Germany, thus posing increased challenge to the security forces there.[163]

German authorities believe the Salafists, who trace their roots to 18th.century Saudi Arabia, want to create a Sunni Islamic caliphate (Islamic Empire) opposed to Western democracy. They consider their brand as 'true' Islam. Hence, they reject any deviation from their 'pure', 'unadulterated' version. German analysis points out that some within the group support martyrdom and the use of violence, and are also fuelling militancy among Germany's socially alienated Muslim youth. These are the "jihadist Salafists" as distinct from the "political Salafists" who opt for spread of ideology as '*dawa*' or mission and profess to abjure violence. However, there is evidence that the distinction between the two categories at times may be quite fluid.[164] Whether 'peaceful' or violent, their ultimate aim is the same, the founding of a *Sharia*-based Islamic caliphate on the graveyard of Western liberalism and democracy. In Berlin, according to the *Verfassungsschutz,* there were 680 known Salafists, of whom about half were violence-prone. The figure had doubled over the last five years, according to Ahmed Mansur, whom we met earlier.[165]

The *Bundesverfassungsschutzbericht 2012* (*BfV Report 2012*) states that "...Germany continues to find itself in the crosshairs of Islamist terrorism, which endangers the security of the country." The *2013 BfV Report* reiterates the same.[166] *BfV Report* of 2014 notes that Salafism continued to be the most dynamic Islamist movement in Germany with 7,000 adherents (compared to 5,500 in the previous year). It further observes that the Salafist scene represented a very important recruitment ground for *jihad*. On 12 September 2014 the German Federal Minister of the Interior, Thomas de Maiziere, banned the activities of the IS. A number of IS followers or supporters were rounded up in Germany that year.[167]

The Syrian conflict has been adding fuel to the fire. The tribulations of the civilian population in that country, the extensive reportage of their woes, especially through the internet, and personal contacts there have been generating and feeding jihadist emotions. According to *BfV* President Dr. Hans-Georg Maassen, at least 450 Germans joined the civil war in Syria,[168] while some 1,800 were in the Middle East as of October 2014. The German Federal Ministry of the Interior updated that information by determining that the total number of Germans travelling abroad to join the Islamic State (IS) or other terrorist organizations rapidly rose from 550 in January 2015 to approximately 700 in June 2015.[169]

The Interior Ministry report of 2014 registers a jump in Maassen's figure. It states that as of early 2015 more than 600 German or German-based Islamists had departed for Syria or Iraq to join the conflicts there. This, according to the report, represented an increase of more than 100% within one year (early 2014: 270 departures).[170] The total numbers remained uncertain, though. In a remarkably similar case, police intercepted several youths from Telengana in India while they were on their way to join the IS in Syria.[171] Maassen told *RBB Inforadio* it was "worrisome" that the number of the Salafists had shot up to around 6,300 from about 2,300 a few years ago.[172] The greater danger is the return of these dangerous men to Germany. The Federal Intelligence Service (*Bundesnachrichtendienst* or *BND*) warned of IS-inspired terror acts in Europe.

According to the *BfV*, in late 2014 there were 25 (2013: 30) Islamist organisations active throughout Germany. Compared to 2013, there was a slight rise in the number of Islamist individuals in Germany to 43,890 (2013: 43,190). This was mainly due to the increase in the number of members or followers of the Salafism in Germany. The Salafists are concentrated along the Rhine-Ruhr region encompassing cities like Bonn and Cologne, and also other big metros like Frankfurt, Hamburg and Berlin.[173]

The Range of Salafism

A RAND Corporation report prepared for the US Department of Defence and dated 4 June 2014 observes that during 2010-2013 the number of Salafi-jihadist groups sympathetic to al Qaeda increased from 31 to 49; the number of jihadist fighters doubled to 100,000; and the number of attacks by al Qaeda affiliates tripled from 392 to roughly 1,000.[174]

It is not known for certain how many Salafists in Germany are connected to international jihadist networks. The Salafist "world view" has spawned an "uncontrolled radicalisation", observes another German government report.[175]

Currently, the Syrian civil war is most attractive to the scene. This is also meant for jihadists from Germany. The former rap musician Denis Cuspert alias Abu Talha al-Almani, originating from Germany, regularly glorified armed combat missions in Syria on video. By glorifying suicide attacks and by expressing on one of his videos—his wish to die a "martyr's" death, he stylised himself as a role model for others. In October 2015 a US air strike helped him fulfil his dream.[176]

But the combat-ready Salafists and their right-wing opponents were further polarising society. That required "appropriate, preventive responses" like banning propaganda organizations like the '*DavaFFM*', '*Islamist Audios*' and '*An-Nusrah*'.[177]

Even before the twin attacks in Paris and the one in Brussels in 2015 and early 2016, respectively, the situation in Europe had looked bad enough. Europol had published a report on 28 May 2014. It maintained that 152 terrorist attacks were carried out in EU member states in 2013; 535 individuals were arrested in the EU for terrorism-related offences; and a total of 150 court proceedings for terrorism charges were concluded for 313 individuals.[178]

The May 2012 elections in France, when François Hollande was elected President, marked the first time that Muslims determined the outcome of a presidential election in a major western European country.[179] Such influence accompanied the growth of Salafism in Europe, including Germany, in recent years. The rapid growth of the salafist ideology in Germany poses one of the greatest threats to national security, according to a German intelligence report.[180] Salafist groups are recruiting and radicalising young Muslims under the guise of doing "mission work", it says. This is an allegation with which far-flung nations, including India, have been living for long. Sometimes, some of the Middle Eastern countries like Saudi Arabia are seen to provide encouragement to such apparently philanthropic work. Among a number of pending cases involving Islamist terrorism prior to the refugee onrush, conspicuous are the ones against four suspected al Qaeda operatives suspected for planning terror act in Germany and the unsuccessful terror act on Bonn's main railway station in December 2012.[181]

Earlier, in April 2011, three Moroccans were arrested in Germany for planning to plant bombs in public places.[182] In September German public prosecutors launched an investigation into Abou-Nagie after he called for violence against non-believers in videos posted on the internet. In his sermons, Abou-Nagie glamorises Islamic martyrdom and says that Islamic *Sharia* law is above the German Constitution. Abou-Nagie has tens of thousands of followers across Germany. Among them are two German Muslim converts-turned-terror suspects trained by Abou-Nagie and arrested in Dover, England. The British border police searched their luggage and found a document entitled "How to Build a Bomb in the Kitchen of Your Mom."[183]

In May 2012 clashes erupted when around 30 supporters of the right-wing political party, *PRO NRW*, demonstrated its opposition to the further spread of Islam in Germany.[184] Over 500 salafists attacked German police with bottles, clubs, stones and other weapons in the city of Bonn, to protest cartoons they said were "offensive." German security is of the opinion that the Salafists believe that in carrying out these acts of violence they are contributing to the worldwide movement to 'defend' Islam.[185] On 5 May 2012 a salafist preacher in Bonn had even threatened the German government that *PRO NRW*-type demonstrations which caricatured Prophet Mohammed would rebound on Germans living in Muslim countries.[186]

What is of additional worry to the Germans, and other Europeans as well, is the phenomenon of "home-grown" terrorists. These are mostly youngsters, raised in Europe, often second or third immigrant generation or simply converts. They are self-radicalised, motivated by salafist/al Qaeda/IS ideology and reject liberal European values.[187] Individuals on their own or in tiny cells can operate autonomously or easily link up with larger networks of veterans and run violent 'errands' for them. The carnages in Paris and Brussels in 2015 and 2016, the San Bernardino mass shooting in the USA in December 2015, the unearthing of jihadist network in eastern India in October 2014[188] followed by the series of murder of secular bloggers in Bangladesh in 2015 and 2016 and the cross-border links of pro-IS elements between Bangladesh and India which are still unraveling in mid-2016 are only a few of the numerous instances of the undeniable power of worldwide appeal of Islamist ideology.

BfV notes that,

> Jihadists originating from Germany have called upon Muslims from our country to leave their familiar environment in order to commit themselves to the jihadist idea, with the actors directly addressing particular individuals or groups of individuals and thus trying to create a feeling of solidarity.[189]

Early instances of the successful indoctrination in Germany are the "*Sauerland-Gruppe*", which perpetrated a violent act in Duesseldorf in 2010, and 22-year Kosovo-born Arid U., who was brainwashed by successful salafist internet propaganda. He committed the first act of Islamist violence on German soil when he killed two US soldiers and wounded two more at the Frankfurt airport in March 2011. He took his life-sentence calmly,[190] which only goes to show the fanatic conviction of self-righteousness that flows from ideological conviction. In September 2015 and February 2016 indoctrinated youths, including a teenage Moroccan girl in the latter case, attacked policemen in Berlin and Hanover, respectively.[191]

Thanks to such proliferation of ideology in the electronic age, countering big, central jihadist organisations alone is not sufficient. For instance, German jihadists mainly publish their propaganda in a decentralized way through social networks or video platforms.[192]

The complexity of Islamist/Jihadist terrorist structures is high. It is both globalised and individualised and appears in different forms: from regional groups associated with the terrorist organisations like IS or al-Qaeda, to diverse networks which are affiliated with these organisations, to 'lone-wolf' actors or micro-groups who/which have often been radicalised by internet publications. The latter make it hard for security agencies to detect at an early stage since they act independently.[193] Self-motivated extremists proliferate and will remain very much active, especially youths itching for action. Mark Owen, a leader of the 24-man US Navy SEAL team which killed Osama bin Laden on 2 May 2011, confirms this in his book.[194]

The German Taliban Mujahideen, however, which sprang up in 2009 following the release of a video, was short-lived after Pakistani forces next year killed its leader.[195] But then, one swallow doesn't make a summer.

Also posing danger are Islamist groups which operate from Germany to replace the governments in their ancestral lands with the Sharia. Examples are the banned *Hizb-ul-Tahrir* (Party of Freedom), the Lebanese *Hezbollah*, the *HAMAS* and the North Caucasian Separatist Movement (*NKSB*). The latter aims at creating a 'Caucasian Emirate' not only in Chechnya but also in the whole of the northern Caucasus in Russia.

Even the apparently mild Islamic community Milli Goerues (IGMG) with the largest number of Islamic groups in Germany, was not above suspicion,[196] though it claimed that it wished merely to ensure better integration on the basis of existing democracy. In actual fact, suspected German intelligence, it strived to strengthen cultural and religious identity, thereby helping forge and spread an Islamist milieu in Germany.[197] It was banned in December 2001.

Different *Weltanschauung*: The Faceoff Quotient

A Gallup Poll in 2011 identified religious and cultural differences across all regions surveyed as the root cause of tension between the Muslim and Western worlds. This was seen as significant in discussions about Islamophobia. While political interests can change and be fleeting, cultural and religious differences are more deeply-rooted within communities. According to the poll, between 16% and 21% of people in France, Germany, and the U.K. said they would not like Muslims as their neighbours.[198] And this was *before* the major attacks in Paris and Brussels more recently.

A larger picture is presented by the report of an anti-racist group *Hope Not Hate*. It lists 920 anti-Muslim organisations and key Islamophobes in 22 countries and notes that such groups are becoming increasingly well-resourced, particularly in the US, where eight foundations have donated substantially since the 9/11 attacks.[199]

According to a study by the Friedrich Ebert Foundation *prior to* the current refugee crisis, 56 percent of Germans considered Islam to be an "archaic religion, incapable of fitting into modern life" and many believed religious freedom for Muslims should be "substantially restricted."[200] Among the reasons were: many third-generation Muslim immigrants are living more strictly than their parents did, in some neighbourhoods Muslim girls were scared to go out without wearing a headscarf, and reports in the German media of ethnic-German men converting to radical Islam and going to wild regions of Pakistan for terror training.

An insightful analysis in *Le Monde Diplomatique*[201] states that the IS and the Islamists are skilfully creating Islamophobia by their atrocious activities so as to sharpen the contradictions between their interpretation of religion and those who oppose it. The more the West retaliates with force, the greater will be the hostility towards it, thereby diminishing and even eliminating "grey zones". The analysis notes that in the past decade-and-half US-led military coalition helped create five failed states (Afghanistan, Iraq, Libya, Syria, and Yemen). Terror groups could thrive in these worlds and attract ever more recruits in their chaos. All of this is like manna from heaven for the Islamic State, the analysis maintains. They seek "the extinction of the gray zone" in our world. In fact, Issue No.7 of the IS's *Dabiq* magazine runs its cover subtitle as "The Extinction of the Grey Zone".[202] Their dream, it continues, is to live in a black-and-white Manichean world of utter religious and political absolutes and clarity (and calamity), while engaging in what American pundits like Huntington calls a "clash of civilizations", as already seen. Karl Popper's classic, *The Open Society and Its Enemies,* also comes to mind. The West's right-wing shift, of course, would put pressure on its large, increasingly isolated Muslim population, which will only play further into IS's (and other radicals') hands.

German Government Response to Refugee Inflow and Integration

The measures taken by the EU and Frau Merkel, especially in cooperation with Turkey, succeeded in stemming the tide of refugees by March 2016 to around 140 a day at the Austro-German border. However, Interior Minister de Maiziere was cautious in stating in an interview whether the high point of the refugee crisis was over for Germany. It would depend, he said, on the continuation of effective measures by Turkey to stem the tide (as had been agreed upon with the EU and Berlin) and efficacious blocking of alternative routes of migration via Libya and Italy.[203]

Berlin stepped up the filtration system to weed out phony asylum-seekers who were actually economic refugees, seeking not protection but better life. On 15 April 2016 21 refugees were sent home back to Georgia since the latter country counted as safe in German view. This was in addition to around 50 more during the first two months of the year. De Maiziere declared that this was a clear signal to all false asylum-seekers to stay back from entering Germany. The disposal of asylum applications was also considerably higher in the first quarter of 2016 (January-March) than in the corresponding quarter of the preceding year.[204]

On the issue of settlement of genuine asylum-seekers, Frau Merkel's coalition government passed a new law on 13 March 2016 based on the resolutions taken by the executive board of the main coalition partner, Merkel's own party, the Christian Democratic Union (CDU), in the month before. For the first time, such a law of integration was passed in post-war Germany. It defined the rights and obligations of the refugees who arrived in the country on a robust legal basis. Underlying the law is clearly the standpoint of the CDU: Germany will help the legitimate asylum-seekers integrate, for instance, by providing subsidised German language and job training courses. But the latter in turn must also demonstrate willingness to integrate. Anyone shirking active participation in integration must face the consequences.[205] It seems that Sarrazin and Buschkowsky's articulations have not been in vain. There are also plans to remove barriers to the labour market and create 100,000 low-paid jobs for asylum seekers. They could also be told where to live so as to prevent formation of migrant ghettos that tend to breed crime and extremism, e.g. the banlieues of Paris or the Molenbeek district of Brussels. However, the Turkish community in Germany, *TGD*, rejected it outright and targeted the Christian Social Union (*CSU*), coalition-leader Christian Democratic Union (*CDU*)'s more right-wing sister party in Bavaria, as the brains behind the new law.[206]

As Interior Minister de Maiziere explained in the interview cited above,[207] every alien, regardless of whether he is a refugee or not, wishing to live in Germany has to undergo the same process, i.e. initially he receives a permit to stay for a fixed period. Thereafter he must be able to demonstrate proficiency in the German language, familiarity with local culture and norms, and the ability to earn a living in order to qualify for a permanent residence status. But the demonstration of those abilities was not checked [in the case of the refugees] and yet he got the permanent residence permit. The new integration law, observed the Minister, will change this privilege for the refugees. The latter will thus be treated at par with other foreigners. The extension of his stay permit will also depend on the situation in his homeland.

Counter-jihad Measures in Germany

Germany's key counter-jihad policy is built on five pillars:

1. Destroying terrorist structures by the increased use of search and investigative measures,
2. Fighting the causes of terrorism by preventing radicalisation processes,
3. Protecting the population and reducing the country's vulnerability,
4. Managing attack consequences in a sustained manner, and
5. Using the opportunities of European international cooperation.

The Hard Approach

In June 2012 German authorities launched a major crackdown on radical Islamists suspected of plotting against the state. The move reflected mounting concern in Germany over the growing assertiveness of Salafist Muslims, who openly state that they want to establish Islamic *Sharia* law in the country and across Europe.[208] The then Interior Minister Hans-Peter Friedrich announced he had banned a Solingen-based Salafist group called *Millatu Ibrahim*. Raids were also conducted in Bavaria, Berlin, Cologne, Hamburg and North Rhine-Westphalia (NRW), among other locations.[209] The latest Europol report states that 99% of the "religiously inspired terrorism" cases were convicted in Europe. In 2013 several plots were disrupted in EU member states, including Germany. In March that year several Salafist suspects were arrested in Germany on suspicion of plotting to murder the leader of the Islamophobic party *PRO NRW*.[210] Europol states that the number of arrested "religiously inspired" terrorists grew from 110 in 2009 to 216 in 2013.[211] Currently jihadist propaganda focuses on two major topics. Firstly, 'individual *jihad*' attacks are encouraged in Western countries, including the EU. Secondly, individuals are incited to participate in fighting and support activities outside the EU.[212]

Among a slew of measures, the respected weekly *Die Zeit* reports that Germany is also taking energetic steps to secure data on air passengers. This despite the fact that the EU Parliament had blocked such measure in 2013 and domestic opposition was critical of the measure. Berlin fears that the Islamic State (IS) militia might sweep in from the Middle East. The 150 jihadists who have so far returned to Germany would also pose palpable danger. In October 2014 three US teenage girls of Somalian and Sudanese descent were arrested at the Frankfurt/Main airport on their way to join the IS in Syria via Turkey.[213] In fact, Salafists supporting the IS, and Kurds opposed to them, are getting into street fights in big German cities.[214] One can imagine how the Germans, punctilious about law and order, feel about it.[215]

In early 2015 the Federal Cabinet decided to halt "jihad tourism". Even the intention to travel to the conflict regions (like Syria) and to join the fight there would attract punishment in future. So might even an announcement of intention to undergo training in a terror camp. Justice Minister Heiko Maas declared that Germany was going to have one of the toughest laws against terrorism in Europe.[216]

But the counter-*jihad* efforts in Germany and elsewhere are sometimes complicated by vote-bank politics, much like in India. French President Hollande successfully cultivated France's nearly six million Muslims to reach power in May 2012. During the campaign, Hollande offered an amnesty to all of the estimated 400,000 illegal Muslim immigrants currently living in France. This was remarkably similar to the long-standing 'vote-bank' politics prevalent in eastern India. He also pledged to change French electoral laws so that Muslim residents without French citizenship would be allowed to vote in municipal elections as of 2014.[217]

Similarly, Germany's then opposition Social Democrats courted disgruntled Muslim voters in a bid to unseat German Chancellor Angela Merkel in the federal elections of September 2013. Peer Steinbrück, Chancellor candidate for the center-left Social Democratic Party (*SPD*), had said earlier at a campaign stop in Berlin on April 3 that he supported the idea of physical education classes in German schools being divided by gender as a courtesy to Muslims. Critics say some German towns and cities are beginning to evoke the sounds and images of the Islamic Middle East.[218]

Other Counter-Jihadist Measures

An Austrian counter-jihadist report explains it all quite succinctly.[219] The main 'risk factors' in Islamism, according to him – and many others in the West – are as follows:

* attractiveness of interpretations of Islamic texts and the resulting radical rhetoric,
* ideological ties of the exponents with pan-Islamist agencies like *al Qaeda* (and now IS),
* radicalisation and recruitment of young Muslims and converts,
* growing readiness to resort to violence, nationally or internationally, within the radicalised spectrum,
* training in terror camps in the Afghan-Pakistan border region, Somalia, Yemen, Mali, Libya, Iraq and Syria,
* potential return of trained elements to Austria (or Germany and elsewhere in Europe).

For a long time there was no terrorism-specific law in Germany. As late as 2009 three new provisions were introduced into the German Criminal Code (Sections 89a, 89b and 91) to counter terrorist threat to the state. They make not only any planning or acts that go against the state illegal but also maintaining contact with terrorist outfits as well as use of the internet or writings preaching propaganda against the state a criminal offence.[220]

Besides the Federal Office for the Protection of the Constitution (BfV), the German Foreign Office (*Auswaertiges Amt* or AA) runs a Federal Committee on Human Rights and Humanitarian Aid. Along with the Armed Services Committee and the Committee on Foreign Affairs it monitors international missions. The Commissioner for Human Rights Issues in the Federal Ministry of Justice (BMJ) represents the government in the European Court of Human Rights and acts as observer to the UN Commission on Human Rights. As a *Rechtsstaat* or law-based state, Germany's constitution upholds through its Articles 1-19 human dignity and rights as inviolable. Article 25 also states that the general rules of International Law shall be an integral part of federal law. Following 9/11 Germany tightened its security laws through two Security Packages (SP I on 8 December 2001 and SP II on 1 January 2002). SP I enabled authorities to ban religious associations advocating violence. SP II tightened the Federal Act on the Protection of the Constitution, among others.[221]

The German Criminal Code does not define 'terrorism'. However, provisions have been fine-tuned to act against serious "criminal offence". The amended acts against international terrorists and organizations relate to people living in Germany as well as those living outside its borders. A number of Financial Action Task Forces (FATF) to track and freeze terrorism-related assets were also created post-9/11.

Since 31 December 2006 an Anti-Terror Data law enables the federal and state intelligence and police units to set up joint databases. Not surprisingly, some critics feared this might encroach upon privacy.[222] In June 2008 the Ministry of the Interior introduced a draft Act on Preventing International Terrorist Threats that would enable the Federal Criminal Police Office (*Bundeskriminalamt* or BKA) to gather information on international terror threats, including remotely accessing computers and intercepting telecommunications.[223]

The core legislation on terrorism remains the penal code and the 2012 Amending Law on the Protection of the Constitution, which renews the anti-terror-laws from 2002 (*Terrorismusbekaempfungsgesetz* or TBG) and 2007 (*Terrorismusbekaempfungsergaenzungsgesetz* or TBEG). The legislation raised the threshold for security authorities to interfere; parliament was given supervisory powers over counter-terrorism; and the preparation of severe state-endangering acts of violence was made a punishable offence.[224]

In December 2015 it was reported that Justice Minister Maas had said the government was investigating 135 domestic cases involving some 200 Germans linked to the war in Syria. Over 700 people were reported to have left Germany to fight alongside terrorist groups like the Islamic State in Syria and Iraq.[225]

A ruling coalition committee took the resolution on 13 April 2016 on further legal and other measures to strengthen the government's anti-terror efforts. The powers of the investigative authorities were widened, and greater intra-EU cooperation on exchange of data welcomed.[226] Seven weeks later, another "anti-terror packet" of measures was passed by the government. These measures would enable the BfV and BND to cooperate more effectively with foreign security agencies. Further, German police agencies were given the power to deploy secret agents to counter impending threats. Buyers of pre-paid cards for their cell phones henceforth will have to produce ID with full address. This would hinder terror suspects to use different cell phones anonymously.[227]

The Instruments of Counter-Jihad

Analytical Resources

The Head of the Federal Chancellery in his function as Commissioner for the Federal Intelligence Services is responsible for coordinating the Federal Government's intelligence services and their cooperation with other authorities and agencies. There are three intelligence services with specific areas of responsibility at the national level, the BfV, the BND and the MAD. These are described below.

The Federal Office for the Protection of the Constitution (*BfV*)

The primary counter-intelligence, and counter-terrorist, agency of Germany is the Cologne-based Federal Office for the Protection of the Constitution (*BfV*), seen earlier. It has around 2,700 members. The Federal Criminal Police Office (*BKA*) looks after terrorism that is international. In November 2014, for instance, it warned of a possible suicide attack in Kabul by a German Islamist convert. Two of the *BfV*'s departments monitor Islamist extremism and terror.[228]

The *BfV*'s annual *Report* of 2013 devotes 48 out of its 212 pages to Islamism, especially Salafism. It observes that Islamism is "a political ideology of recent times and stands for the ideologisation of the Islamic religion."[229] Another *BfV* analysis maintains that Islamism rejects Western-type democracy with its elections, equal rights for males and females and the entire value-system on which democracy is based for political purposes.[230] As seen earlier, the borderline between 'non-violent' and jihadist Salafism may not be watertight. Noteworthy here is the fact that although

Salafists reject 'modernism', they have little scruples in using 21st. century technology like the internet to spread their ideology.

In January 2014 Dr. Hans-Georg Maassen, President of BfV, told *rbb Inforadio* it was "worrisome" that the number of the Salafists had shot up to around 6,300 from about 2,300 a few years ago.[231] The 2014 *Annual Report* noted that there was "a slight rise in the Islamist following in Germany to 43,890 (2013: 43,190) due to the increase in the number of members/followers of the Salafist movement in Germany in particular." Europe continues to be the target of Islamist terrorism, it observed.[232]

The Federal Intelligence Service (*Bundesnachrichtendienst* or BND)[233]

The BND has been operating since 1956, has its headquarters in Pullach near Munich and an office in Berlin-Lichterfelde. According to its website, a new headquarters is currently being built in the centre of Berlin in walking distance to the federal chancellery and the parliament. Its President is Gerhard Schindler. However, reports floated in April 2016 about the impending replacement of Schindler by Bruno Kahl, a confidante of conservative Finance Minister Wolfgang Schaeuble of the CDU party.

Schindler was found to be feeding confidential data to the US National Security Agency on European allies. The BND is currently facing a demand for reform. It is speculated that Schaeuble, who is opposed to too much of restrictions on the BND not least because of the threat posed by Islamist terrorism, had intervened with Chancellor Merkel.[234]

The BND warned of the danger posed by the return of the jihadists from Syria and other volatile countries to Germany, a perceived danger we already noted. It warned specifically of IS-inspired terror acts in Europe. The Salafists are concentrated along the Rhine-Ruhr-Schiene region encompassing cities like Bonn and Cologne, and also other big metros like Frankfurt, Hamburg and Berlin.[235] It is the largest metropolitan area in Germany with over 11 million inhabitants.

In early December 2015 German Vice-Chancellor Sigmar Gabriel demanded that Riyadh should cut money flowing to the Wahhabis. He stressed that the Saudi regime was funding mosques known for radicalizing the Muslim population, including in various communities in Europe. "Wahhabi mosques all over the world are financed by Saudi Arabia. Many Islamists who are a threat to public safety come from these communities in Germany", he declared.

The basis for his statement was a no-nonsense BND report. The German government downplayed it. But according to the media, the BND had warned about Saudi Arabia adopting a destabilizing role. The previous cautious diplomatic stance of older leading members of the royal family, said the agency, was being replaced by an impulsive policy of intervention and a more aggressive foreign policy since King Salman ascended to the throne in January. The Saudis reportedly offered to build 200 mosques for the Syrian refugees in Germany while themselves giving them a wide berth.[236]

Military Counter-Intelligence Service (*Der Militärische Abschirmdienst* or *MAD*)[237]

MAD is part of the Federal Armed Forces and performs tasks in Germany and abroad relating to the protection of the constitution under the responsibility of the Federal Ministry of Defence. Its tasks include gathering and evaluating information on extremism and terrorism. Its President is Dr. Christof Gramm.

Besides these three intelligence agencies which deal with Islamist terrorism among others, there are other police agencies as follows.

The *Bundeskriminalamt (BKA)*[238]

Police jurisdiction in Germany lies mostly with the 16 German states. However, coordination is an imperative. The *BKA* provides such coordination. It .is the federal investigative police agency of Germany, directly subordinated to the Federal Ministry of the Interior. Founded in 1951, it is headquartered in Wiesbaden in the state of Hesse, and maintains major branch offices in Berlin and Meckenheim near Bonn. It is headed by Holger Münch since December 2014. Its personnel number over 5.500 and are from 70 different professions. In the 1970s and 1980s it was preoccupied with tackling the Red Army Fraction (RAF) terrorists. Since mid-1980s it became increasingly involved in fighting the growing international drug business and other forms of organised crime. In January 2005 a new Department of International Coordination was set up.

The agency's main tasks include coordinating cooperation between the federation and state police forces; investigating cases of international organized crime, terrorism and other cases related to national security, and counterterrorism. Its missions include:

Coordinating cooperation between the federation and state police forces (especially state criminal investigation authorities) and with foreign investigative authorities,

collecting and analyzing criminal intelligence, managing the INPOL (*de*) database of all important crimes and criminals,

investigating cases of terrorism or other areas of politically motivated crime, as well as narcotics, weapons and financial/economical crime.

On 31 July 2006 there was a failed attempt to bomb trains in western Germany. Two Lebanese youths living in Germany were arrested, one of them in Tripoli in north Lebanon. The *BKA* handled the case in cooperation with the Interpol and Lebanese police.[239]

The Common Terrorism-Defence Centre (*GTAZ*)[240]

In late 2004 the *GTAZ* (*das Gemeinsame Terrorismusabwehrzentrum*, or Common Terrorism-Defence Centre) had already been founded in Berlin. In November 2012 the *GTAZ* was further expanded to include both terrorism and right-wing extremism and was called the Common Extremism and Terrorism-Defence Centre. This reform was meant to ensure better coordination among all the agencies involved.[241]

The *GTAZ* is not an autonomous authority but a joint co-operation and communication platform used by 40 internal security agencies (including the *BKA*). The *GTAZ* has no head, but representatives of the participating agencies co-operate on an equal footing. Key to the success of the *GTAZ* is the co-operation between intelligence and police institutions and actors. The prerequisite for their co-operation 'under one umbrella' was the setting-up of two separate pillars, i.e. the *Nachrichtendienstliche* and the *Polizeiliche Informations- und Analysestelle* (*NIAS* and *PIAS*, respectively the Intelligence and Police Information and Analysis Unit). The *NIAS* and *PIAS* have several working groups (WG) that serve different objectives. Besides dealing with current cases and threat prognoses, they also draw up medium- or longer-term analyses. The working groups include threat assessment, operational information exchange ("Information board"), potential Islamist terrorists, de-radicalisation, and Intelligence Board. Success in counter-terrorism depends on the cooperation of various intelligence and police organs.

In addition, measures are taken concerning the law on foreigners and on coordination of preventive and repressive requirements aimed at long-term effectiveness. The *BfV* claims that the successful investigations into the *Sauerland* Group, which led to the prevention of a terrorist attack in Germany, have shown that the *GTAZ* and *NIAS* structures are well functioning and efficient.[242] Interior Minister Thomas de Maiziere at a *GTAZ* convention in Berlin on 28 October 2014 stressed the need for "close, efficient and successful" coordination and cited the *GTAZ* as a "model of success" "admired" also abroad.[243] A European Centre for Combating Terrorism was also set up on 1 January 2016 to strengthen the powers of the Europol in its fight against terrorism.[244]

Four Islamic State (*IS*) refugee-terrorists were arrested on February 4, 2016 at three 'asylum centres' across Germany. The arrests pre-empted a major IS attack in Berlin and other unspecified cities in Europe. The Berlin attack was scheduled to take place at the famous Alexanderplatz in the city, a major tourist hub next to the city's iconic TV station tower. Two of the arrested had obtained jobs working for a tourist bus company on the

Alexanderplatz. The cell leader, a 35-year-old Algerian, was arrested on Thursday in an "asylum home" in Attendorn in North Rhine-Westphalia. He had entered Germany in autumn 2015 as a "refugee" through the "Balkan route" and was registered as a "refugee" in Bavaria.

Yet another refugee-terrorist was arrested from another "asylum home" in Hannover but this was unconnected with the arrests in Berlin. The Hannover arrest, the police said, was linked to an *IS* cell in Molenbeek in the Belgian capital of Brussels. The police also raided an 'asylum centre' in Isernhagen in the state of Lower Saxony, where a former restaurant has been converted into "refugee accommodation." Earlier, on January 22, 2016, police had raided a "refugee house" in Recklinghausen in search of *IS* terrorists linked to Paris attacker Walid Salihi. Nine non-whites were arrested in that raid. Salihi had used at least seven different identities in Germany to disguise his movements and to swindle seven "asylum seeker" allowances out of the state.

The Salihi case shows that not every aspect of counter-terrorism may have been optimal in the deluge of asylum-seeking refugees. Earlier, the head of the German police union, Rainer Wendt, had warned that the massive numbers of non-white refugees had made it impossible to check them all, and that only a fraction had even been registered. According to reports, the *IS* leader already had an arrest warrant issued for him by the Algerian government for receiving military training in Syria. The warrant had been circulated to Interpol, but the German authorities apparently failed to act upon it.[245]

In sharp contrast to the overall success of inter-agency cooperation within *GTAZ* and *GIZ* we shall presently come to the latter – is the Burdwan blast case in India. Clandestine bomb-making and indoctrination activities of the *Jamaat-ul-Mujahideen Bangladesh (JMB)* on Indian soil were unearthed by India's central government police and intelligence agencies in the state of West Bengal neighbouring Bangladesh. This followed an accidental explosion on 2 October 2014. The state police agencies reportedly had been dragging their feet and even trying to sabotage investigation by the centre's National Investigation Agency. West Bengal's police reportedly ignored earlier alerts provided by the centre revealing a total lack of not only coordination but also cooperation.[246] Similar subversive activities by IS or IS-related cells have been reported from Bangladesh adjoining West Bengal, especially the killing of several secular bloggers and liberal-minded people there. The terrorists who attacked a popular Dhaka café, noted earlier, that killed over 20 people in the beginning of July 2016, mostly foreigners, may have had links again in adjoining West Bengal in India. This linkage and the very likely role of IS, directly or indirectly, was being investigated by Indian and Bangladeshi intelligence and police agencies. The IS has gloated over these actions.[247]

In mid-2016 media reports announced that several people had been nabbed by National Investigation Agency (NIA), India's counter-terrorism agency, created following the Mumbai carnage of 2008 that same year. The persons, arrested in Hyderabad in India's south, included their IS recruiter.[248]

Web Jihad and The Joint Internet Centre (*GIZ*)[249]

Extremists have been increasingly using the internet for propaganda, as a think tank, mentor and as a means of communication. De Maiziere at the *GTAZ* convention in Berlin in 2014 highlighted the power of the internet. It has not only helped, he stated, to promote radical propaganda. Even beyond, the net eased mobilisation of "over 4,000 people" in a violent confrontation between the so called "hooligans" and the Salafists "within a short time" on 26 October evening that year in Cologne.[250] Videos with powerful emotional content showing the plight of Syrian "brothers and sisters" in the civil war there appeal to the true believers for help ranging from the financial to joining the fighting.

Hence, the Joint Internet Centre, or *GIZ*, was set up in 2007 in Berlin to monitor and analyse websites containing Islamist content. Besides coordination and cooperation within the GTAZ, the various security agencies also cooperate within the framework of the Joint Internet Centre. The *GIZ* also maintains regular exchange with the competent federal state authorities. The multiple authorities represented within *GIZ* have been tasked with monitoring, assessing and analysing publications with Islamist and jihadist contents posted on the internet. This enables the government to identify extremist and terrorist structures and activities on the internet at an early stage. To this end, the various linguistic, technical and expert competences of the authorities involved are centralised.

The German concern about jihadist misuse of the internet is by no means unique.

The Dutch intelligence service, *AIVD,* reports similar experience. "Social media has made it possible for a person to go far more quickly from being a passive recipient of jihadist propaganda messages to a sympathizer and then a supporter. . .it has taken on the characteristics of a swarm (in the group behavior sense)," it observes. In India the Islamists with links to Bangladeshi terror outfits have used skype to communicate.[251] In October 2014 several of the European states held talks with US internet giants like Microsoft and Twitter on the widespread use of the net by the terrorists. Indeed, Robert Hannigan, the Director of the UK's eavesdropping spy agency GCHQ, sharply criticized the internet majors as providing the terrorists with "command and control networks of choice". Writing in *The Financial Times,* he adds, "The Islamic State of Iraq and the Levant (IS) is the first terrorist group whose members have grown up on the internet. They are exploiting the power of the web to create a jihadi threat with near-global reach."[252]

The techniques adopted for counter-terrorism,[253] including that of the jihadist variety, encompass special investigation techniques or SIT. SIT embraces undercover operations, use of informers, 'controlled delivery', i.e. illegal transport runs over national borders monitored by prosecution, 'planned monitoring', i.e. observation ranging from 24 hours to one month and, with judicial permission, longer. Other methods include electronic surveillance, bugging, interception of communications, searches, 'hot pursuit' under Article 41 of the Convention applying Schengen Agreement, deployment of agent provocateurs, and so forth.

Action: Special Forces/Commandos

Among the various police units meant to fight crime, there are special ones which are dedicated to fighting terrorism. In the forefront are *GSG-9* (*Grenzschutzgruppe*-9 or Border Protection Group-9), the *SEK* (*Spezialeinsatzkommandos* or special operation command, a SWAT unit), the KSK (*Kommando Spezialkraefte* or special forces command), and the newly created *BFE+* (the *Beweissicherungs- und Festnahmeeinheit* plus or "evidence collection and arrest unit plus"). Of course, there are other units like the *MEK* ((*Mobiles Einsatzkommando* or mobile operations command) as well.

The famous *GSG-9* was formed in response to the Munich Olympics massacre of 1972, when Palestinian Black September terrorists penetrated the German Olympics village and massacred eleven Israeli athletes along with a German police officer. Set up within that very month of the outrage of 5 September in 1972, the *GSG-9* carried out so far over 1,700 operations during the next 40 years, losing only three men and resorting to firearms only six times. It is based in leafy Sankt Augustin near Bonn. It operates quietly and is for the most part invisible. Its high-profile action, though, came in October 1977 when it faultlessly executed a seven-minute rescue mission of a Lufthansa passenger jet hijacked to Mogadishu, the capital of Somalia, with zero casualties among both the passengers and its assault team. Another, more recent, action was its rounding up of the *Sauerland* group of terrorists in Germany, mentioned earlier. Besides fighting terrorists with its snipers, paratroopers, divers and other specialised troops, it also tackles organised crime and other serious criminal activities where heavy physical action is needed.

The number "9" of the *GSG-9* arose from the fact that when the group was formed, there were already eight border units of the BGS (*Bundesgrenzschutz* or federal border security force), and this was the ninth. The name stuck.[254]

The *KSK* was formed in 1996 to provide a dedicated Special Forces unit for Germany. Hitherto, different aspects of counter-terrorism had been assigned to different agencies. While counter-terrorism had belonged to the domain of *GSG-9*, reconnaissance came under the Army's *Fernspaeher* (Long Range Reconnaissance), maritime duties had been assigned to the Navy's *Kampfschwimmer* (Combat Swimmers), and direct action to the *Sonderwaffenbegleitkompanien* (Special Weapons Escort Companies). Upon the official activation of *KSK* on April 1, 1997, all such roles were incorporated into it. *KSK* may also be used in German to mean "no one sees them coming" ("*keiner sieht sie kommen*")!

The differences between the *SEK, MEK, GSG-9* and the *KSK* are as follows.

The *SEK* are the special response units of the German state police forces. The main missions of *SEK* units are to serve arrest warrants and to deal with barricaded suspects. Hostage sieges, kidnappings and raids also belong to their missions as well as other scenarios like personal security detail for VIPs or witnesses.

The *MEK* is a mobile tactical force deployed to track moving suspects and at times even to arrest them. It is equipped with special monitoring and tracking equipment.[255]

The *GSG-9* is a also a police force but at the federal/central government level. As already mentioned, it is part of the federal border security force or *BGS*, like the FBI Hostage Rescue Team. It is responsible for particularly serious attacks, like the one at the Munich Olympics in 1972 (before its advent) or the 1977 plane hijacking in Mogadishu.[256]

The *KSK* is a military unit like the British SAS. It is branch of the German military for the execution of foreign operations for crisis prevention. Since the German constitution bars from the military from deploying at home, the *KSK* cannot operate within German territory but only aboard. Previously, the *GSG-9* undertook operations abroad, like the Mogadishu venture, but ever since the KSK was created, the latter was assigned that responsibility. The *GSG-9*, like any police force, is confined to operating at home. However, the *BGS*, its parent organisation, does operate abroad though in purely police functions and with the consent of host nations, e.g. in protecting embassies, VIPs, taking over peacekeeping operations from the army like in Kosovo, etc. The *KSK*, estimated at 1,100 personnel, is deployed primarily in hostile foreign environments like Afghanistan.[257] Despite the tactical and operational capabilities to resolve hostage situations, *KSK* is primarily a military unit with military missions—not like the *GSG-9* counter-terrorism division. *KSK* also includes the so-called "Hostage Rescue Team" capable of solving diverse and complex tasks involving hostages.[258]

Two months following the multiple Paris attacks in November 2015, Interior Minister de Maiziere commissioned a study on the preparedness of German security forces for such situations. The finding: *There is room for improvement*. The report said that agents lacked the training and equipment to deal effectively with well-armed terrorists like those in Paris. The result was the setting up of the new unit called the *BFE+(Beweissicherungs- und Festnahmeeinheit plus* or "evidence collection and arrest unit plus").[259]

The *BFE+* is a unit to launch large-scale simultaneous manhunts, for instance, after a spate of multiple attacks like in Mumbai in 2008 and 2011 or in Paris more recently, when terrorists retreat into hiding. This has drawn attention to a gap because the normal federal police supposedly cannot do this. According to criminologist Rafael Behr, the upgrade mainly serves as a psychological reassurance for the public. Five batches of 50 personnel each would be located in five regions, starting with Blumenberg near Berlin, a total of 250 security operatives. Says Joerg Radek, deputy chairman of the German police union *GdP*:

> We are faced with a new type of perpetrator, one that has been to war and knows how to handle military weapons. Until now, an attack would be carried out, then the

> perpetrator would go into hiding. But now perpetrators are moving, they are dynamic, and several attacks take place at different locations at the same time.[260]

Security expert Wolfgang Petri, not unlike Behr, remains skeptical of the creation of the new force. "We don't need another unit," Petri told the German press agency *dpa*. He says that the money would be better spent reinforcing and equipping existing units. He argues that it is impossible to create an effective special forces unit in such a short period of time: "It's pure window dressing", says he.[261]

It may be noted here that units like the *SEK* are direct attack forces, and are not necessarily trained to conduct large-scale, sustained manhunts. The *BFE+* is meant to fill that gap. They are to offer support to *GSG-9,* as well as federal and state police, during large anti-terror operations. The *BFE+*, along with the *GSG-9,* are expected to be fully equipped with military-standard weapons – since the military cannot deploy at home, as noted above – that the normal police units lack in order to fight the heavily-armed terrorists.

The Soft Approach

Counter-radicalisation (number two of the five pillars of Germany's counter-jihad measures depicted above), or deradicalisation, is of utmost importance. It includes a multi-dimensional approach utilising civic education and religious-political dialogue as well as an active policy of integration. The Federal Agency for Civic Education, the Federal Agency for Migration and Refugees, and several civil society projects are key instruments. This strategy, inclusive of the prevention policy, has been continuous since 2001.[262]

Germany deployed teachers since fall 2014 who brief Islamic teachers working in the country on the basic values of German society. Many Islamic Imams and other Islamic teachers hitherto came from countries like Turkey who spoke no German but preached in mosques in their native tongue. Germany is now determined to change this scenario. German as the medium of religious instruction is being encouraged as a tool promoting integration. Also, it has the advantage of supervising the nature of the teachings, thereby minimizing or eliminating radical ideas.

Refugee Radio *Funkhaus Europa* (*FHE*) runs information programmes for refugees in English and Arabic. It provides latest news on the situation and political discussion in Germany; information about healthcare services, legal matters, integration and volunteering.

A perceptive Japanese report from March 2015, however, is skeptical about the effectiveness of these measures. Many Islamic organisations in Germany, it says, are not participating in the curriculum supervision programme. Also, it questions whether the passing on of Western values and norms to true-believers would cut ice. Even then, says the reporter, this is the first such experiment with Islam in Europe.[263] According to Ralf Jaeger, Minister of the Interior of the state of North-Rhine Westphalia, attempt was already underway as of November 2014 to counsel youths to prevent them from falling for Salafism (Islamism), for instance, at the counseling centre in Bochum.[264]

The German-Islamic Conference (*Deutsche Islamkonferenz* or *DIK*)

As Dr. Ehrhart Körting, Senator for the Interior and Sport, summed it up, German socio-political order is based on a clear separation of religion and state. The Islamists preach their brand of religion with a politico-ideological motive and completely deny such separation. This is the key problem faced by Germany.[265] And, one may add, by most other open, liberal democratic societies.

With typical Teutonic thoroughness, Germany has adopted a two-pronged strategy to fight the jihadist menace. Berlin supplements its 'hard' approach to tackling Islamist terrorism with an ideological—soft—approach. After all, the jihadist ideology, like most ideologies, aims at capturing the minds of the impressionable, particularly the youth. Hence, ideas are needed to counter dangerous ideas. The state runs the German Islamic Conference (*DIK*) since 2006 to address better integration of Muslims.[266] The main event ('Plenum of 30'), held annually, aims at promoting a dialogue with the Islamic minority and assuring them of their rights in a Western democracy while trying to isolate the extremists devoted to violence in the name of religion. A number of task-group sessions also take place during the year. Since 1 January 2012 the Federal Office for Migration and Refugees (*BAMF*) runs an advisory for those who wish to seek help from radicalism.[267]

The *DIK* aims to improve social and religious integration of Muslims, e.g. by establishing Islamic religious teaching in schools and training of Imams in Germany. This is to encourage students to learn their religion better. The aim seems, among others, to afford the students a sanitised perspective of the value of their religion without falling for a 'distorted' jihadist version. The *DIK* is not primarily concerned with Islam as religion involving theological issues but is rather a dialogue between the state and the Muslims to coordinate issues of coexistence and socio-religious integration. It aims at reaching an understanding on the binding nature of the German legal framework and value system of Germany's constitution. All the Muslims and their organisations participating in the DIK have declared that they do not demand a parallel Islamic law.[268]

More than 2000 individual Muslim communities form the nucleus of Muslim life in Germany. Some of these are organised into nationwide umbrella organisations, of which the predominantly the Turkish *DITIB* and the multi-ethnic Muslim Council (*IRD*) are the largest. Together with two other umbrella organisations, both were affiliated with the Coordinating Council of Muslims in Germany (*KRM*) in 2007. Among the roles of these umbrella organisations is the representation of Muslim interests within the German-Islamic Conference.

However, it should be noted that Cem Özdemir, who is of Turkish origin, and Volker Beck of the Green Party in their paper published at the end of 2015 allege that the four most important Muslim organisations of Germany (*DITIB, Islamrat, ZdM* and *VIKZ*, not counting the Alewite Community of Germany or *AMG*) are not really religion-oriented but rather groups of compatriots with political goals, and some of these have connection with mentors in Ankara and the Muslim Brotherhood. Further, they represent only a fraction of the Muslims in Germany. So, the authors maintain, to favour these organisations because they are thought to represent the majority of the millions of Muslims living in Germany in the Coordination Council serves neither religion nor integration.[269]

Finally, the Initiative Security Partnership is another institution that is supposed to improve the cooperation between Muslims and German security authorities.[270]

Other 'soft' measures include the launching of a *Bundestag* (German Parliament) programme of offering scholarships to invite students from Arab universities to visit Berlin in 2016 and watch how the Parliament functions. The *Suedwest Rundfunk (SWR)* radio's forum called *"Das Islamische Wort"* (the Islamic word), started way back in April 2007, was the first such forum offered with audio and text on its home page. The *ZDF* TV also offers from that year a *"Forum am Freitag"* (Forum on Friday) for Imams and other Islam experts to discuss Islamic affairs which is open also to non-Muslims.[271] Indeed, France was reportedly following suit in terms of overhauling its teaching of secularism to counter radicalism.[272] The Stresemann Foundation operates a website called *islamdebatte.de* (Islam Debate) to throw light on the religion, the points of friction with Muslim culture in Germany/Europe and their clarification, and makes available key documents related to these problems.

With Islamist terrorism, droves of Muslims are being killed too, whether in Syria, in Iraq, regions of Africa, Afghanistan, Pakistan or elsewhere. Extremists have ruthlessly persecuted the Yazidis, the Shias, the Kurds, Alewites and all kinds of ethnic groups within Islam, not to speak of non-Muslim populations. The Syrian civil war which has generated so many millions of refugees and so much of misery is a war among Muslim groups.

To be sure, there are Turks and Middle Eastern people of distinction who have publicly opposed the extremism displayed by radical Islamists. They range from media reporters like Abdul Ahmad-Rashid, a German-Afghan conducting *ZDF* TV's programme 'Forum on Friday' devoted to discussion on Islam, as seen before, authors like Rafiq Schami, Syrian-born (though of Syriac-Christian descent) and Ahmad Mansour, a self-described "Arab-Israeli", living in Germany, to Mahbuba Aykat, a school teacher there, to Cem Oezdemir, chair, Alliance 90/Green party of Germany, to the Grand Imam Sheikh Ahmed al-Tayeb of Cairo's al-Azhar University, Egypt's top Islamic institution. Sheikh Ahmed has called for a radical reform of religious teaching to tackle the spread of Islamic extremism.[273] Somewhat paradoxically, although Saudi Arabia is widely noted as a patron of hardline Islam, its Foreign Minister Adel al-Jubeir also declared opposition to the IS brand of radical Islamism.[274] Reacting to the German intelligence (*BND*) report of December 2015 cited above, which is critical of Riyadh for financing Islamic radicals, the Saudi Embassy in Berlin stated, "Like Germany, we are part of the anti-Islamic State coalition and fighting side by side against terror."[275] To a question whether Muslim groups and spiritual leaders could not do more to distance themselves from IS, Interior Minister de Maiziere gave a terse reply stating that any open critique of IS murders would definitely help.[276]

Denouement

The set of refugee-related problems staring Germany in the face as of 2015-16 comes in the following context.

A massive effort was already underway through the 1990s to integrate former East German states following reunification and the subsequent onrush of ethnic Germans from the disintegration of the Soviet Union and its bloc. These often included peasant elements who were in name German but otherwise had little in common with the modern Germans, including linguistic difficulties. Meanwhile, the problem of integration of a large and long-settled Muslim minority – largely Turkish – continued. This older problem of minority integration is now exacerbated by the huge avalanche of refugees – mostly Muslim – descending upon Germany as well as other countries of Europe. The rapid growth of the Muslim component of the country's population entails an even greater challenge of integration. That challenge is further compounded by terrorism, both home-grown and sneak-in types. 'Multi-culturalism', or "multi-kulti", as the Germans call it, seems to have failed. Instead, as Buschkowsky warned, "the other society", mentioned earlier, which is largely resistant to integration, seems to have already taken shape. The addition of refugees is further reinforcing it.

The media have not sufficiently highlighted the key role of smuggling rings operating under the very nose of various governmental authorities. In the meantime, while the refugee crisis seems to have been brought under control somewhat, their alien culture, which reinforces that 'other' society, has understandably given rise to xenophobia, in Germany and the rest of Europe. Fear that the mainstream Germans – and

Europeans—might be swamped and lose their own cultural identity in the obstinate growth of the 'other' culture has triggered the spectacular rise of right-wing extremists throughout Europe. 'Brexit', or the UK referendum of 23 June 2016 in favour of quitting the EU, largely stemmed from the fear of a refugee invasion (though, in Britain's case, largely from the poorer European states).The term *PEGIDA*, standing for 'Patriotic Europeans Against the Islamisation of the Occident', is itself revealing of this phenomenon. Germany, as indeed much of Europe, today faces the unenviable task of management of the increasing polarisation of society on the growing Muslim minority issue.

But the exo-European religion and related culture does not, in the European perspective, halt at merely running parallel to the mainstream religion and culture. While that itself is ultimately unpalatable, it is the chiliastic, religious ideology-fuelled mindless violence that finds its apparent sustenance in the 'other', parallel society and even doctrinally connects and spreads to the mainstream that causes the maximum worry.

The incidence of the lack of integration does not lie purely on one side. Host Europeans like the Germans, the French, the Belgians, the Dutch and others have tended to neglect their 'guest workers' (*Gastarbeiter*, the German term for foreign workers, largely Turkish in Germany, who helped rebuild the country after World War II), mostly relegating them to more menial jobs. Often they are concentrated in ghettos like the French *banlieues* or suburbs, especially around Paris, Molenbeek in Brussels or Kreuzberg in Berlin. The 'guest workers', in their turn, are inclined to stubbornly cling to themselves, to their communities, cultural values and religious practices to the extent that often turn out to be detrimental to better integration in their host societies. Even while a worker may be skilled and enjoy a decent income, his relatives who arrive are frequently low-skilled or unskilled and equipped with little education. They do not speak the language of the host country, nor are they inclined to learn it. Without language skills, they cannot pick up new skills. Poverty remains their hallmark. They fail to sufficiently open up to the needs of living in a different culture. For instance, there are many migrants who have been living in Germany for a long time and yet cannot speak German. The Germans maintain that they do not have the drive to integrate with their host nation. The guests, on the other hand, lament discrimination and lack of opportunity. The net result has been increasing alienation of the guests from their hosts.

Over the past three-and-a-half decades the Soviet military intervention in Afghanistan, followed by 9/11, the US-led or inspired wars in Afghanistan, Iraq and Libya and other turmoils in Africa and the Middle East – most notably Syria – dramatically increased Islamist terrorism. *Al Qaida*, the *Taliban, Boko Haram*, the *IS* and their numerous affiliates, or like-minded but independent groups, sprang up and spread spectacular violence. Their chief target was the West, topped by the USA and followed by its European allies which supported US war efforts against Muslim states. Germany counts among those NATO allies; its troops deployed in Kunduz in northern Afghanistan from 2003 while its experts trained Afghan police personnel. More recently, in November 2015 Defence Minister Ursula von der Leyen announced that Berlin was preparing to back French military strikes against the IS by providing Tornado reconnaissance jets, a naval frigate, satellite images and aerial refueling. It would also bolster its military training mission in northern Iraq, where it was helping Kurdish forces battling IS militants, German MP Henning Otte said, reported BBC (http://www.bbc.com/news/world-europe-34927170, 26 November 2015)

Like all open, democratic societies Germany has to steer between Scylla and Charybdis of retaining its liberalism and constitutionally guaranteed freedoms versus the increasing need to effectively counter growth and acts of terrorism that imperatively need encroaching upon those freedoms. A Nazi Germany under Hitler, a Stalinist Russia or a Maoist China could dictate to people and use ruthless police power unrestrained by legal niceties and constitutional constraints. But a modern democracy has to respect those niceties and restraints to remain an open society. Berlin faces an unenviable role; whether that of a Minotaur or Theseus trying to escape the labyrinth remains to be seen.[277] The democratic state *ipso facto* thus willingly undergoes auto-constraints, ties its own hands for the sake of safeguarding individual liberty. The terrorists are aware of this and take full advantage of it.

It is also interesting, as noted in passing earlier, that though the Islamists, whether *al Qaida,* the *IS* or others, preach a seventh century religious ideology, and profess strict conservatism in their life style, they have no hesitation in using the fruits of ultra-modern technology like the internet and the media, the computer, communications equipment, or arms and other gadgets and methods. German authorities have repeatedly noted their frequent use of the internet and the computer to spread their ideological propaganda via slick modern products like videos and online magazines. Their media-savvy operators have thereby scored astonishing success, as the spate of attacks and mass killings, worldwide, in recent times have testified.

It is remarkable that their ideology continues to have a great deal of appeal, both in the West and in the East. The Islamists easily recruit fighters mostly from among youths, whether in Germany, rest of the West or India and elsewhere. Those who suicide-bomb themselves or do the actual fighting and die are mostly in their teens or twenties. These appear to be youths, largely disgruntled, dissatisfied and frustrated, for any number of reasons (broken homes, unemployment, feeling of discrimination or injustice, drop-out or criminal backgrounds, etc.).

The impact of modernization and globalization means that traditional societies suffer a breakdown. But something broken does not automatically guarantee that a new and viable substitute will replace it. Globalisation involves rapid socio-cultural changes generating a turmoil of values that often leaves the individual, particularly youths, confused and uncertain. Add to this the natural proclivity of youth towards romanticism and its spirit of adventure, towards non-conformism, even defiance and the longing for recognition and respect. Joining a terror outfit provides a sure outlet for all these inclinations plus gives a disgruntled youth, particularly one who is without a firm goal in life, a feeling of belonging and a sense of purpose.

Hence, it is small wonder that even youths from relatively affluent strata of society, be it in the West or in the East, are often found to be terror perpetrators masquerading as religious zealots. Some of them were described by their surprised relatives and acquaintances as 'regular' boys, not invariably religious, with fondness for material goodies of life. Some even attended modern, elite institutions and were outwardly as 'modern' as any. Several of the 9/11 assailants trained to fly in South Florida. One of them, the Egyptian Mohammed Atta, had studied architecture at Cairo University, and had continued his studies at the Technical University of Hamburg, Germany. A *Washington Post* report of 12 April 2016 states that prosecutors noticed that a terrorist cell consisted of "a web of predominantly young, European-born men quietly radicalised within Europe".[278] As an expert observed following the 2 July 2016 terror attacks in Dhaka, "The shock value for the radical groups of recruiting educated, affluent people is huge. The government will never suspect them. The intelligence agencies will never suspect them. Because these boys were never under any kind of surveillance."[279] More on that attack later.

So, it is alienation of a different sort and not just poverty or *madrassa*-borne bigotry that can explain the radicalisation of youths of this type. Often, a father figure, a Messiah, appears in the life of the disgruntled youth, seems to understand his dissatisfaction and empathises with him. This could happen in the virtual world as well. The Messiah provides simple, clear-cut solutions that seemingly cut through complex problems that have him worried, and promises him the millenarian paradise—in exchange for strict discipline and absolute obedience. This provides a huge psychological relief. The youth, being impressionable, succumbs to the charm of what he considers a noble goal worthy even of the supreme sacrifice of martyrdom. The 'lone wolf' type sublimates his frustration and social, political or economic resentment by finding an ideological justification. By discharging his psychotic overload he reaches a cathartic ecstasy.

Indeed, Russia's security chief Alexandr Bortnikov, quoted earlier, stated that the "formation of an aura idealising individual terror is unfortunately achieving its goal, which is seen in the growing trend toward high-profile actions by suicide bombers. . . .The glorification of suicide attackers and the creation of a faith martyr halo around them" posed a continuing threat.[280]

Psychological experts at the University of California-San Diego have developed the Terrorist Radicalization Assessment Protocol (TRAP-18), an analytical tool with 18 indicators that would warn of a 'lone wolf' terrorist in the making.[281]

As one analysis concludes:[282]

> The old-fashioned image of the fundamentalist recruiter has taken a beating. The new recruiters are tech-savvy men who look for potential recruits on social networking forums, coaching institutes, neighbouring cafes and private colleges. And they are men who had been similarly recruited . . . The recruiters are also young men, many in the age group of 18-24 years . . .
>
> [Following the carnage of over 20 people at a fashionable café in Dhaka on 2 July 2016] . . . the police discovered that three of the young terrorists belonged to influential families of Bangladesh . . . [Recent reports stated that] three Bangladeshi boys, again from influential families . . . were believed to have gone to Syria . . .

It is the same picture in widely separated regions. In Berlin, as in Bangladesh, the social media like *Facebook* and others, the internet and the digital world, play a crucial role in this process of conversion and recruitment. When Kashmir's popular young militant, the 22-year old Burhan Wani was killed on 8 July 2016, an earlier report on the state's militancy by former police Inspector General Abdul Ghani Mir, gathered fresh traction. The Mir report had determined that the surge in the Kashmiris' access to social media was directly responsible for the spread of Wani's rock star-like popularity, especially among the youths. Consequently, Wani's death unleashed massive turbulence in the Indian state.[283]

Besides rapid diffusion of ideas, today's virtual, digitised world has also created a tumescent void in the inner lives of a large number of youths who live in it and have little of the rich, traditional social and cultural life of their parents or grandparents. In a globalising world of high mobility, torrential change of mores, values and relationships, they often suffer from an identity crisis and sometimes loneliness. Paradoxically, the rapid technological changes of the 21st. century are forever widening the gap among people even as they bring them physically and – more often – virtually together.

The smart recruiters know of this inner vacuum. They use the same digital world that creates the void to fill in that void. They spread their strong audio-visual messages among the gullible and provide the choice of a rock-steady religio-ideological identity. Only such a psychological explanation in the context of today's digital age can help explain why apparently normal youths from economically well-off families, whether in the West or in the Third World, are turning terrorists. Of course, other region-specific problems also add fuel to the fire, e.g. demand for Kurdish, Kashmiri, Chechen or Uighur independence, the eternal Palestinian question, numerous issues in the Syrian-Iraq cauldron, etc. As do individual proclivities to crime and other idiosyncrasies.

According to the *BfV*, the German counter-intelligence agency, of the extremists modern freely use modern audio, video and text messages. The *IS*, says Germany's Interior Ministry report, has shown a remarkable degree of professionalism in not only producing and spreading its propaganda via video messages but also via social media-accounts.[284] Their weapons are also products of the modern age which they profess to detest. This confirms the preceding analysis although its context is far-away Bangladesh in South Asia.

The successful spread of Islamism/Salafism is amazingly akin to ideological influence through the ages. The French Revolution, Marxism in Russia, Nazism in Germany, Fascism in Italy, and Maoism in China are examples of ideologies strewn along the path of history. The Cold War, of which more soon, was ideologically-driven. In India there was the ideology of nationalism used against the British rulers. So we had Khudiram, Kanailal, Bagha Jatin, Binoy, Badal, Dinesh, Surya Sen, Netaji,

Bhagat Singh and numerous others who sacrificed their lives for the noble ideological cause of securing the freedom of Mother India. The same devotion bordering on fanaticism could be found in the 1960s and 1970s, worldwide. University campuses like Sorbonne, California-Berkeley, Tokyo, and, nearer home, Calcutta and Jadavpur were up in arms against the US military intervention and bombing in Vietnam. In the simultaneous pro-Mao Naxalite movement of those decades, some of the brightest students in West Bengal, among them quite a few from rich families, got down to the business of making and throwing bombs, even fought it out with the police and got killed. Paradoxically, some of them subsequently found their niche in the USA – their ideological enemy No. One – and happily settled down there. It was Maoist ideology, as interpreted locally, that had lured the Naxalites to a millenarian utopia.

Youth and idealism seem to go hand in glove together. There are many things undeniably wrong with the so called 'modern' civilisation and its offshoot culture. The quotidian excesses of capitalism in a 'post-Christian' West which promotes greed as a virtue, and the consequential mindless consumerism is one. The syndrome of the rich-getting-richer-and the poor-poorer, the impact of globalisation, the 'permissive society' involving vastly increased erotic content in movies, plays, novels, commercial advertising and the media and their impact on our daily lives; increased divorce, promiscuity, premarital sex, extramarital sex, unnatural sex, spousal abandonment, and out-of-wedlock births; declining birth rates and diminished parental commitment to the welfare of children; and related to these developments, growth of juvenile delinquency and organsied crime, psychological depression, and mental disorders of every description tend to lead to a spiritual vacuum that encourages abuse of drugs, crime and worse. *Herbert Marcuse's* 'one dimensional man', critique of the modern industrial society, comes to mind.

Pitrim Sorokin interpreted the contemporary Western civilization as a 'sensate' civilization dedicated to technological progress and prophesied its fall into decadence and the emergence of a new ideational or idealistic era.

Alvin Toffler's work in *Future Shock* described the high impact of social change accompanying hectic modernisation as "culture shock" that forces the "culture-shocked" person, like the soldier in war or victim of a disaster, to grapple with unfamiliar and unpredictable events, relationships and objects. "Information overload", i.e. unfamiliar streams of inputs that an individual and society must process at a rate difficult to cope with may, he suggests, lead to confusion and breakdown.

Oswald Spengler's Faustian West is confronted by the Magian, Islamic East. The individualistic Western striving, the apotheosis of the individual, the 'I', as architecturally symbolized by the tall, slender church spire is rejected by the "We" of the Magian, Islamic—and socialist—world, with its emphasis on the collective, as represented by the dome of the mosque.[285]

Samuel P. Huntington's modern classic, *The Clash of Civilizations,* is partly a result of the dislocating effect of modernisation. While the latter process breaks up traditional societies, that does not automatically entail that it spawns a new, modern and viable structure. Many other studies of modernisation (e.g. by Daniel Lerner, Samuel P. Huntington's concept of 'political decay', etc.) have pointed to the dislocating effects of modernisation. Rebellion by the youth, encouraged actively by ideology, is a natural outcome.[286] Islamists provide an apparently sure and tempting roadmap. As Huntington's soothsaying determined way back in 1993 in his essay on the *Clash*:[287]

> It is my hypothesis that the fundamental source of conflict in this new world will not be primarily ideological or primarily economic. The great divisions among humankind and the dominating source of conflict will be cultural. Nation states will remain the most powerful actors in world affairs, but the principal conflicts of global politics will occur between nations and groups of different civilizations. The clash of civilizations will dominate global politics. The fault lines between civilizations will be the battle lines of the future.

Huntington, writing at a time when the Cold War had just ended, had mentioned 'ideology' in the sense of communism vs.

capitalism. To the present author, the idea of the clash of civilisations is indisputable in the post-Cold War era. That era is defined by the Taliban, al Qaida and the Islamic State. But the civilisation they represent is not static. They are actively promoting it locally, regionally and globally. There is demonstrably an active, at times even aggressive, propensity to promote it and subvert other civilisations. Even several instances of ethnic Europeans undergoing religious conversion have been seen, as in the case of Denis Cuspert *alias* 'Deso Dogg', the Afro-German rapper-turned-jihadist.

To this extent their proselytising mission serves an ideological purpose not dissimilar from the communist ideology and its sponsors.

Youth dissatisfaction is also fed by political, social and economic problems ranging from big, international issues (like the issue of a Palestinian homeland) to other regional or local ones (Chechen, Kashmir, Xinjiang, Tibet, Bangladeshi secular bloggers).

Much of the Cold War between the capitalist West and the socialist East had been on ideological grounds. Thus, a number of brilliant British university students, some of whom later occupied important, even sensitive, British government posts, turned out to be spies – the so called Cambridge Five – working for the Soviet Union. The motivation, again, was ideological conviction. From the West's standpoint, there was a perceived external threat – the Soviet bloc's military might – and an insidious threat, from home-grown communist sympathisers.

So, the danger the West is facing today does have certain parallels to the Cold War decades. To be sure, the threat of a war imposed from outside is absent. The terrorists, outside IS-held territory, hardly run states and armies in the conventional sense. And whatever territory might be under IS's control, the latter is hardly in a position to launch conventional military attacks on the West. It is having a hard time in the face of combined assault from the US, its allies – though some are dubious – and Russia. But the insidious threat of Bivishanas – the *Ramayana's* villain Ravana's brother who sided with the enemy, Ramachandra – or home-grown terrorists, and Trojan Horse refugee sneak-in types, is palpable.[288] And the relentless manifestation of this bewildering threat is a testimonial to the power of ideology, albeit based on religion.

One challenge before Germany today is how to prevent the coagulation of the refugees into fresh ghettos. This in turn will depend on the degree of success of integration. The great challenge now, therefore, is to draw the refugees—and the entire Muslim minority—into the mainstream of Germany's life. If this can be achieved, it would not only choke off the breeding ground of terrorism but also provide a gerontologically challenged Germany—as well as the rest of Europe—with not only a fresh but also safe labour force. Provided, of course, appropriate education is not only imparted but also willingly received. As noted earlier, Germany has already taken the initiative to offer integration courses, including language teaching, and stresses its expectation that the new arrivals also show eagerness to grasp this opportunity.

Conventional wisdom is being put to novel test. It is generally held as axiomatic that exposure to a different culture 'liberates' a person from the shackles of the culture of his forefathers. Imparting modern education to him frees him from irrational beliefs and endows him with a rational, scientific outlook. A second generation immigrant who is born, brought up and educated from his childhood in a different cultural environment and in a language different from his mother-tongue is expected to naturally adapt to his host country's ways. But that 'liberating' effect seems to have failed in the case of the Europe-born terrorists. It was a Dutch Muslim of Moroccan descent, born and socialised in Europe, who murdered the filmmaker Theo van Gogh in Amsterdam in November 2004 for making a film on the plight of Muslim women. On August 5, 2012 British journalist John Cantlie expressed astonishment at the number of "disenchanted young Britons" fighting in Syria in an account of his experience published in *The Sunday Times*. Elton Simpson, 30, was one of the two gunmen who tweeted loyalty to the IS and opened fire on police blocking their way to a cartoon exhibit and contest depicting the prophet Muhammad near Dallas in May 2015.[289]

It remains to be seen who is correct, Sarrazin or Buschkowsky. For Sarrazin, as we have seen, the Middle Eastern/North African minorities in Germany are a gone case, genetically inferior, therefore incapable of making progress in learning and unsuitable for living in a modern society. Modern education would not help them better integrate. Buschkowsky, on the other hand, holds extending education as key to upliftment, integration and progress. On this point there seems to be a convergence between his views and those of Nobel laureate Indian economist Amartya Sen.[290]

In any case, Berlin's choice is limited. Once accepted into German society, there might as well be an all-out effort at integration. The Germans are expected to be poised to tackle their task with characteristic Teutonic thoroughness.

Notes

1. 'Do not come to Europe,' Donald Tusk warns economic migrants, http://www.theguardian.com/world/2016/mar/03/donald-tusk-economic-migrants-do-not-come-to-europe#top, electronically accessed 9:26 PM Indian Standard Time (IST), 3/9/2016. All times below are those shown in the respective web site unless indicated otherwise.
2. Rachel Herp Tausendfreund, "Europe's Immigration Problem", (editorial foreword), Internationale Politik, Deutsche Gesellschaft fuer Auswaertige Politik, Berlin, vol. 12, No.4, July/Aug.2011, p.1; Pinak Ranjan Chakravarti, "The Syrian Ceasefire is risky and fragile game", The Telegraph, Kolkata, 26 April 2016, p.9.
3. As of March 2016, over 4.5 million people fled Syria since the start of the conflict, a further 6.5 million people were internally displaced inside that country. "Syria: The story of the conflict", http://www.bbc.com/news/world-middle-east-26116868, 11 March 2016. Electronically accessed on 03 April 2016, 7.30 pm IST. Details of the workings of the IS inter alia in Brian Dodwell et al., The Caliphate's Global Workforce: An Inside Look at the Islamic State's Foreign Fighter Paper Trail, Combating Terrorism Center at West Point,United States Military Academy, April 2016,https://www.ctc.usma.edu/v2/wp-content/uploads/2016/04/CTC_Caliphates-Global-Workforce-Report.pdf.Electronically accessed on 18 April 9.06 pm IST.
4. The full term is *Bundesamt fuer Verfassungsschutz*, or *BfV*, meaning Federal Office for the Protection of the Constitution. In the USA, Presidential candidates, among others, were engaged in a debate over the nuances of those terms. The National Public Radio reported in June 2016 that Republican Donald Trump and many on the right say it's "radical Islam." But Democrat Hillary Clinton used a different term: "radical Islamism."Last year President Obama explained his view on the issue: it was incorrect, he said, to use the term "radical Islamic terrorism" to describe groups like the self-proclaimed Islamic State or al-Qaida. Such groups, he said, did not represent Islam, nor were their leaders religious leaders. "We are not at war with Islam," Obama said. "We are at war with people who have perverted Islam." Radical Islam Or Radical Islamism? It Depends Whom You Ask, http://www.npr.org/2016/06/14/482011041/radical-islam-or-radical-islamism-it-depends-who-you-ask, June 14, 2016.Electronically accessed on 25 June 2016, 7:58 AM IST.

5. Soeren Kern, "Salafi-Jihadists: "A Persistent Threat" to Europe and America", http://gatestmeininstitute.org/4355/salafi-jihadists-threat,%2013%20June%202014; Wolgang Guenter Lerch, Frankfurter Allgemeine, "Die suendigen westlichen Werte", review of Behnam T. Said, Hazim Fouad (eds.), "*Salafismus*". *Auf der Suche nach dem wahren Islam*, Herde, Freiburg im Breisgau, 2014, 25 July 2014, p.10; Dirk Baehr, *Der deutsche Salafismus*, http://www.grin.com/de/e-book/173076/der-deutsche-salafismus, (excerpt). See also Foreword by Dr.Hans-Peter Firedrich, Federal Minister and Member of Parliament, 2nd. Paragraph, Bundesverfassungsschutzbericht 2012; and BfV Report 2013, p.28, Berlin; BfV Report 2013, Fakten und Tendenzen, Kurzzusammenfassung, Berlin, p. 21, http://www.verfassungsschutz.de.
6. www.verfassungsschutz.de,, *Focal topics of jihadist online propaganda*, .pdf document. Electronically accessed on 16 April 2016, 9.06 pm IST.
7. Donald Tusk, president of the European Council, had been negotiating a deal whereby asylum-seekers would be sifted on arrival in "hotspots" in Greece and Italy, and those rejected would be sent back to Turkey. The new scheme, championed by the German chancellor, Angela Merkel, is a more ambitious arrangement—all boat-people would be sent back to Turkey and processed there. These people will be treated as"irregular migrants", meaning all those outside normal transit procedures, i.e. without documentation. This would avoid turning Greece into a refugee camp, offer a stronger disincentive to illegal migration and ensure that Europe grants protection to the most deserving, not those most able to pay people-smugglers. But problems remain in implementing the agreement, problems posed by 70-odd EU preconditions, such as introduction of biometric passports, delays in forwarding the funds promised and Turkey's dubious credential as a democracy under President Recep Tayyip Erdogan that keeps it out of the coveted EU membership. See Endnote 1 above, and "A messy but necessary deal", http://www.economist.com/news/leaders/21694536-european-bargain-turkey-controversial-offers-best-hope-ending-migrant, Mar 12th 2016, accessed same day, 8 pm IST; www.bbc.com/news/world-europe-35763101, electronically accessed 9 March 2016, 9 pm IST.
8. The International Organization for Migration (IOM) estimates that more than 1,011,700 migrants arrived by sea in 2015, and almost 34,900 by land. This compares with 280,000 arrivals by land and sea for the whole of 2014. The figures do not include those who got in undetected. "Migrant crisisis: Migration to Europe explained in seven charts", http://www.bbc.com/news/world-europe-34131911, 4 March 2016, electronically accessed 13 March 2016, 8.15 p.m. IST.
9. President Assad and many of the governing party and security officials belong to the secretive Shia sect known as the Alawis, or Alawites. Even though minority, the Alawites run the government in the Sunni-majority country. Unbridled hostility towards the minority Alawi population is a major reason for the civil war in Syria. Many Alawis believe their only

choice is to kill or be killed. "The Alawis", BBC Radio 4, http://www.bbc.co.uk/programmes/b01qdtql. Electronically accessed 30 June 2016, 7.36 pm IST.

10. A turn for the better seemed to be in the offing in March 2016. President Vladimir Putin ordered Russian military to withdraw most of its fighting forces from Syria, signaling an end to Russia's five-and-a-half month air campaign. UN-brokered talks were also going on in Geneva on Syrian peace, though the future of Moscow-supported Assad government there remained dubious as of mid-March 2016. "The Latest: UN envoy says Syria talks to continue on Monday in Geneva; important Kerry-Lavrov meeting coming up", Associated Press March 18, 2016. http://www.usnews.com/news/world/articles/2016-03-18/the-latest-russian-planes-back-syrias-battle-for-palmyra. Electronically accessed on 19 March 2016, at 2:57 p.m. IST.
11. **"The Sunni-Shia Divide",** http://www.cfr.org/peace-conflict-and-human-rights/sunni-shia-dividep33176#!/?cid=otr-marketing_url-sunni_shia_infoguide, electronically accessed on 19 March 2016, 7.50 p.m. IST.
12. Paul Adams, "Turkey caught in overlapping security crisisises", http://www.bbc.com/news/world-europe-35801176, 14 March 2016. Electronically accessed on 20 March 2016, 3.p.m. IST.
13. Jennifer Rankin, "Turkey outlines 'one for one' plan to tackle Syrian refugee crisisis", http://www.theguardian.com/world/2016/mar/07/eu-offers-another-3bn-to-turkey-at-emergency-migration-summit, 7 March 2016 22.34 GMT; HUMEYRA PAMUK AND GABRIELA BACZYNSKA, **"EU, Turkey seal deal to return migrants, but is it legal? Or doable?"** http://www.reuters.com/article/us-europe-migrants-turkey-davutoglu-idUSKCN0WK0QQ. Electronically accessed on 19 March 2016, 8.26 p.m. IST. Ankara's central objective -- visa-free travel for Turks to Europe by June -- would still depend on Turkey meeting 72 long-standing EU criteria; "Text:EU MigrantDealWithTurkey",http://www.nytimes.com/reuters/2016/03/18/world/europe/18reuters-europe-migrants-eu-draft.html, REUTERS, MARCH 18, 2016, 10:48 A.M. E.D.T.
14. **"Turkey roundtable: War at two fronts?** "http://www.aljazeera.com/indepth/interactive/2015/08/turkey-roundtable-war-fronts-150803123130959.html, 04 Aug 2015 11:06 GMT, electronically accessed on 15 March 2016, 8.11 p.m. IST.
15. *The Economist* online, op.cit.
16. Stefan Lehne,et al.," The Roots of Europe's Refugee Crisisis", http://carnegieeurope.eu/2015/10/01/roots-of-europe-s-refugee-crisisis/iie3, October 1, 2015. Electronically accessed 12 March 2016, 8.30 p.m. IST.
17. Maybrit Illner, "Kampf gegen IS-Terror: Bomben allein reichen nicht", zdf.de, 20 November 2015, 10.15 pm CET.

18. "Poland's new PM says the country will not accept an EU quota of 4,500 refugees in the wake of the Paris terror attacks", http://www.dailymail.co.uk/news/article-3333233/Poland-s-new-PM-says-country-not-accept-EU-quota-4-500-refugees-wake-Paris-terror-attacks.html, Mar 13th 2016, 2 a.m. . See also Neil Buckley in London and Henry Foy in Warsaw, "Poland's new government finds a model in Orban's Hungary", http://www.ft.com/cms/s/0/0a3c7d44-b48e-11e5-8358-9a82b43f6b2f.html, January 6, 2016 5:39 pm.
19. Patrick Strickland, ' Refugee crisis: Hungary sends more troops to border', http://www.aljazeera.com/news/2016/03/refugee-crisisis-hungary-sends-troops-border-160309134453267.html, 10 Mar 2016 03:17 GMT; Rita Pálfi, ' Hungary's prime minister suspects "masterplan" is behind refugee crisisis', http://www.euronews.com/2015/11/13/hungarian-prime-minister-talks-about-leftist-masterplan-behind-refugee-crisisis/,3/11/15, electronically accessed 0.31 pm IST. More than 386,000 migrants passed through Hungary in 2015 before its borders were closed in October .An organiser of the Paris attacks "recruited" some migrants from Budapest's main train station, Hungarian officials have said. Migrant crisisis: Hungary challenges EU quota plan in court, 3 December 2015.http://www.bbc.com/news/world-europe-34998615.
20. Simon Kent, "Now Austria Plans To Build A Fence To Thwart Europe's March Of Muslim Migrants",http://www.breitbart.com/london/2015/10/28/now-austria-plans-build-fence-thwart-europes-march-muslim-migrants/, 28 Oct 2015, electronically accessed 13 March 2016, 3.40 a.m. IST. The report goes on to state that "Slovenia, the main entry point into Austria, also said it was ready to build a fence, meaning the two countries will follow Hungary in trying to seal their frontiers..." As a *The Guardian* commentary observed, "With Sweden and Denmark reintroducing border controls in a new Europe of razor-wire fences, fear of mass immigration and homegrown terror, obituaries are already being written", Ian Traynor, "Is the Schengen dream of Europe without borders becoming a thing of the past?" 5 January 2016, 12.15GMT,http://www.theguardian.com/world/2016/jan/05/is-the-schengen-dream-of-europe without-borders-becoming-a-thing-of-the-past?
21. "Migrant crisisis: Hungary challenges EU quota plan in court",3 December 2015, http://www.bbc.com/news/world-europe-34998615. Electronically accessed 13 March 2016, 9.16 p.m.IST.
22. BBC.com, "Migrant crisisis ...", op.cit.
23. "'We know our reality': Why Poland is cool on the EU refugee crisisis,", http://www.csmonitor.com/World/Europe/2016/0310/We-know-our-reality-Why-Poland-is-cool-on-the-EU-refugee-crisisis,, Sara Miller Llana, **Staff writer** Monika Rębała, **Correspondent** MARCH 10, 2016,electronically accessed 11 March 2016, 9.18 pm IST.
24. "Osteuropäer weisen Asyl-Reformpläne der EU-Kommission zurück", http://www.nzz.ch/international/aktuelle-themen/fluechtlingskrise-osteuropaeer-weisen-asyl-reformplaene-der-eu-kommission-zurueck-ld.18071, 4 May.2016, 3:47 pm CET.

25. David Crouch, "Sweden and Denmark crack down on refugees at borders", http://www.theguardian.com/world/2016/jan/03/sweden-to-impose-id-checks-on-travellers-from-denmark, 4 January 2016 11.39 GMT.
26. Crouch, theguardian.com/, op.cit.
27. Berlin Social Science Center, WZB, "German Public Opinion and the Refugee Crisisis: Mechanisms of Support and Opposition", https://www.wzb.eu/en/node/39651.
28. Ian Traynor,"Germany to push for compulsory EU quotas to tackle refugee crisisis", https://www.theguardian.com/world/2015/oct/23/refugee-crisisis-germany-push-compulsory-eu-quotas, 23 October 2015, 11.48 GMT.
29. The attacks in Paris on the night of Friday 13 November by gunmen and suicide bombers hit a concert hall, a major stadium, restaurants and bars, almost simultaneously - and left 130 people dead and hundreds wounded. "Paris attacks: What happened on the night" **http://www.bbc.com/news/world-europe-34818994**, 9 December 2015, Electronically accessed on 16 March 2016, 9.20 IST. "Three co-ordinated teams" were believed to have been behind the attacks, according to Paris chief prosecutor Francois Molins. Dozens of women were harassed and groped in the heart of Cologne on New Year's Eve by a large group of men between 15 and 35 years old. They appeared to have migrant backgrounds. Many seemed to be from North Africa. According to police, some 90 complaints had been filed by 5 January 2016 morning and that a quarter of the complaints made were related to sexual harassment or groping, with many others pertaining to theft of purses, wallets and mobile phones. "New Year's Eve Attacks: Dozens of Women Sexually Assaulted in Cologne",http://www.spiegel.de/international/germany/cologne-shocked-by-sexual-assaults-on-new-years-eve-a-1070583.html, Electronically accessed on 16 March 2016, 9.45 p.m.IST. Cologne's Imam, Sami Abu-Yusuf, reacted in an interview with Russia's RENTV that the women themselves had invited the attacks because they were dressed half-naked and wore perfume. Later, he detracted his statement saying he had been quoted out of context. Www.noz.de, 22 January 2016, 8.43 pm CET.
30. **MELISSA EDDY**, *"German Sentenced to 14 Years for Stabbing Mayoral Candidate in Cologne"*, http://www.nytimes.com/2016/07/02/world/europe/henriette-reker-stabbing-cologne-germany.html?emc=edit_tnt_20160701&nlid=67256862&tntemail0=y&_r=0, JULY 1, 2016. Electronically accessed on 02 July 2016, 9.11 pm IST.
31. "So reagiert das Ausland auf Koeln", https//de.nachrichten.yahoo.com. Electronically accessed on 08 January 2016, 6.50 pm IST.
32. Melanie Amann, et al., "The Rise of Germany's New Right", http://www.spiegel.de/international/germany/refugee-crisisis-drives-rise-of-new-right-wing-in-germany-a-1067384.html, December 11,2015 06:22 PM CET; Markus Feldenkirchen, "A Brutal New Germany:

What's Happening to My Country?"http://www.spiegel.de/international/germany/editorial-on-anti-refugee-sentiment-in-germany-a-1062442.html, November 12, 2015 06:19 PM.

33. Melanie Amann, et al., op.cit.; "Islamophobe Movement Returns With a Vengeance", http://www.spiegel.de/international/germany/deep-concern-over-return-of-anti-muslim-pegida-protests-a-1057645-druck.html, October 14,2015 11:46 AM CET.

34. "2015 Paris Terror Attacks Fast Facts", http://edition.cnn.com/2015/12/08/europe/2015-paris-terror-attacks-fast-facts/, March 21, 2016,2023 GMT.

35. See usatoday.com,14 Nov.2015, the Financial Times (ft,com), 14 Nov.2015, Wall Street Journal (wsj.com), 16 Nov.2015, the Voice of America (voa.com), 17 Nov.2015, and Spiegel.de 8 Jan.2016. Electronically accessed on 16 March 2016, 5 p.m. IST.

36. "Chaos and Violence: How New Year's Eve in Cologne Has Changed Germany", http://www.spiegel.de/international/germany/cologne-attacks-trigger-raw-debate-on-immigration-in-germany-a-1071175.html, January 08, 2016 06:43 p.m.

37. "maybrit illner spezial" mit dem Thema "Streitpunkt Flüchtlinge - drei Wahlen, ein Thema", 10 March 2016, http://www.zdf.de/maybrit-illner/maybrit-illner-5990162.html. Eelctronically accessed 12 March 2016, 9 pm IST.

38. "Krankschreibung statt Abschiebung: Das Geschäft mit ärztlichen Attesten", http://www.spiegel.de/sptv/magazin/. Electronically accessed on 4 April 2016, 6:32 AM IST

39. Of course, many Germans resist inoculation for various reasons. Video: https://de.nachrichten.yahoo.com/masern-ausbruch-deutschland-gesundheitsminister-kritisiert-impfgegner-062851889.html, Electronically accessed on 4 January 2016, 6:59 PM IST.

40. "Kein Fall fuer zwei", Der Spiegel, No.42, 10 October 2015, pp.25-27.

41. Stefan Wagstyl, "Schäuble warns of refugee 'avalanche' in dig at Merkel",http://www.ft.com/intl/cms/s/0/379d4afe-8930-11e5-9f8c-a8d619fa707c.html, November 12, 2015 1:01 pm. Frau Merkel explained her policy of patiently coping with the refugee problem in cooperation with the rest of EU in "Angela Merkel bei Anne Will - das vollstaendige Interview", https://www.tagesschau.de/multimedia/video/video-161245.html, 29.02.2016 01:09 am CET, and in Hubertus Volmer,""Gute Argumente" gegen die AfD.Die kritische Frage stellt Merkel selbst",http://www.n-tv.de/politik/Die-kritische-Frage-stellt-Merkel-selbst-article17612866.html, 03. May 2016. Electronically accessed on 04 May 2016, 9.15 IST. N-tv. reports that Merkel argued that if states like Turkey, Jordan and Lebanon could handle millions of refugees each, surely the 500 million-strong EU could afford to admit one million refugees a year. Especially because Europe is economically strong and the refugees are to go home once the conflicts stop. Syria, she says, is EU's neighbour; from past experience of refugee onrush to Germany during

and following reunification, Germany received much help from neighbours. Her view is that neighbours must help each other.

42. Wagstyl, op.cit.
43. Hungary registered strong reservations on the quota issue. See note 4.
44. "No breakthrough at German 'refugee crisisis meeting' as opposition grows",1 Nov, 2015 14:04,https://www.rt.com/news/320405-germany-refugee-crisisis-meeting/; DAVE KEATING, "Dissent threatens Merkel's refugee plans", BERLIN, 10. NOV 2015, 09:13,https://euobserver.com/beyond-brussels/131034;"Politicians challenge Merkel's refugee policy pleading 'nearly exhausted resources", 03.10.2015,http://www.dw.com/en/politicians-challenge-merkels-refugee-policy-pleading-nearly-exhausted-resources/a-18759765.
45. "Migrant crisisis", Migration Policy Centre, European University Institute, Florence, http://www.migrationpolicycentre.eu/migrant-crisisis/
46. See Carnegieeurope.eu, note 6.
47. "The Latest: UN envoy says…", op.cit.
48. Oliver JJ Lane, Hungarian Border Fence So Effective Illegal Immigrants Are Now At Pre Migrant Crisisis Levels, http://www.breitbart.com/london/2015/10/29/hold-hungarian-border-fence-so-effective-illegal-immigrants-are-now-at-pre-migrant-crisisis-levels/,29 Oct 2015, electronically accessed 13 March 2016, 3.33 a.m. IST.
49. Wagstyl, op.cit. The Schengen Agreement started functioning from 1995. Named after a Luxemburg village where the agreement was signed in 1985, it counts 26 states as its members while eight potential members are in the pipeline. the Schengen area is not to be confused with the EU. "Schengen Area Countries List", http://www.schengenvisainfo.com/schengen-visa-countries-list/. Electronically accessed on 03 April 2016, 8.32 IST.
50. Http://www.dutchnews.nl/news/archives/2015/09/european-refugee-crisisis-dutch-to-bring-in-more-border-spot-checks/, September 14, 2015, electronically accessed on 17 March 2016, 9.35 IST.; http://www.euronews.com/2016/02/24/belgium-turns-back-migrants-and-refugees-at-border-with-france/, 24/02 13:53 CET; http://www.express.co.uk/news/politics/637143/Migrant-crisisis-France-prime-minister-Manuel-Valls-Europe-can-t-accept-every-refugee,19:04, Fri, Jan 22, 2016, electronically accessed on 17 March 2016, 9.40 IST.
51. Stefan Lehne,"HOW WILL THIS CRISISIS IMPACT POLITICAL STABILITY IN EUROPE?", op.cit.
52. Jan Techau, "Was Europe Prepared?" in STEFAN LEHNE, et al., The Roots of Europe's Refugee Crisis, http://carnegieeurope.eu/publications/?fa=61465. Electronically accessed on 12 April 2016, 8.45 pm IST.
53. Tom Parfitt, "Russia spies keep tabs on 'living bombs', The Telegraph, Kolkata, 29 July 2016, p.3, reprinted from The Times, London. Bortnikov addressed the conference on 27 July 2016. https://www.rt.com/news/

353506-fsb-suicide-bombers-russia/. Electronically accessed on 29 July 2016, 8.14 pm IST.

54. "Intelligence-speak for a terrorist who is a native of the target nation", who can move about the country, cross its borders and penetrate institutions without causing eyebrows to be raised. Stella Remington, ex-Director-General of MI5, the British internal security service, "At Risk", Reader's Digest Select Editions, Sydney, 2005, p.294 (condensed version).
55. Epeius in Greek mythology had built the Trojan horse that destroyed Troy insidiously.
56. A typical example was the legal controversy between the FBI demanding access to unlocking an Apple-created iPhone of the two attackers in a December 2015 terrorist attack in San Bernardino, CA.
57. Dabiq, Issue13, Foreword, p.3. https://www.clarionproject.org/factsheets-files/Issue-13-the-rafidah.pdf.Electronically accessed on 04 April 2016, 1.40 am, IST.
58. Video Polittalk, ZDF TV. "Feinde im eigenen Land.Was tun gegen den IS-Terror?" http://www.zdf.de/maybrit-illner/maybrit-illner-5990162.html, 31. März 2016, 22:15 CET. Electronically accessed on 4 April 2016, 8:05 PM IST.
59. RUKMINI CALLIMACHI, ALISSA J. RUBIN and LAURE FOURQUET, "A View of IS's Evolution in New Details of Paris Attacks", The New York Times (NYT), http://www.nytimes.com/2016/03/20/world/europe/a-view-of-ISs-evolution-in-new-details-of-parisattacks.html?emc=edit_th_20160320&nl=todaysheadlines&nlid=67256862&_r=0, MARCH 19, 2016, electronically accessed on 3/20/2016, 7:45 PM IST.
60. Video news, heute.de, quoting AFP and AP. Electronically accessed on 29 December 2015, 9.15 pm IST; bbc.co.uk/radio/players/bbc_world_service. Electronically accessed on 31 December 2015, 7.40 pm IST.
61. "From Paris to Brussels: Why the attacks are linked", http://www.bbc.com/news/world-europe-35879401, 23 March 2016. Electronically accessed on 23 March 2016, 8.45 pm IST; Peter Allen, Corey Charlton, "Paris terrorist ringleader bragged he entered France among a group of 90 jihadis and claimed the migrant crisisis had made it easy for them to travel freely across Europe", http://www.dailymail.co.uk/news/article-3431479/Paris-terrorist-ringleader-bragged-migrant-crisisis-easy-Islamists-travel-freely-Europe-reveals-woman-led-police-him.html. Electronically accessed on 23 March 2016, 9.05 pm, IST.
62. "Paris attacks: Key suspect Abrini arrested in Brussels", http://www.bbc.com/news/world-europe-36000407; "Belgium attacks: Mohamed Abrini 'admits being man in the hat'", http://www.bbc.com/news/world-europe-36005709. Electronically accessed on 10 April 2016, 01.30 am, IST.
63. "Paris and Brussels bombers' links uncovered", http://www.bbc.com/news/world-europe-35879401, Electronically accessed on. 10 April 2016, 2.00 am IST. "Hatte Abaaoud Kontakte zu Deutschen?" http://www.tagesschau.de/inland/abaaoud-deutschland-101.html, 28.November.2015 11:36 am CET.

64. TATP, a crystalline powder, is easy to make and hard to detect, but is also incredibly unstable. In fact, all it takes is a firm tap to explode TATP with a force that's about 80% as strong as TNT. Hence its ill- reputation as "the Mother of Satan" among terrorists who make it. See http://www.techinsider.io/paris-attack-tatp-chemical-bombs-2015-11. Electronically accessed on 25 March 2016, 12.40 pm IST.
65. Tom Whitehead, Con Coughlin, "Isil exploiting migrant routes to smuggle jihadists back to Britain using fake documents", http://www.telegraph.co.uk/news/worldnews/islamic-state/12123333/Refugee-routes-main-tactic-for-Isil-terrorists-to-get-in-to-Europe-and-launch-attacks-British-intelligence-officials-fear.html,26 Jan 2016, 9:30 pm GMT.
66. " IS Exploiting Refugee Crisisis To Smuggle Terrorists Into Europe", http://www.ndtv.com/world-news/IS-exploiting-refugee-crisisis-to-smuggle-terrorists-into-europe-1270698, January 27, 2016 19:04 IST.
67. U.S. Department of Justice. Office of Public Affairs. Attorney General Holder Urges International Effort to Confront Threat of Syrian Foreign Fighters, July 8, 2014, http://www.justice.gov/opa/pr/attorney-general-holder-urges-international-effort-confront-threat-syrianforeign-fighters; Daniel L. Byman and Jeremy Shapiro, "Managing the Foreign Fighter Threat," The Brookings Institution, January 14, 2015, http://www.brookings.edu/blogs/markaz/posts/2015/01/14-byman-shapiroforeign-fighters; UN Department of Public Information, "Security Council Unanimously Adopts Resolution Condemning Violent Extremism, Underscoring Need to Prevent Travel, Support for Foreign Terrorist Fighters," SC/11580, September 24, 2014, http://www.un.org/press/en/2014/sc11580.doc.htm; SYRIAN REFUGEE FLOWS. SECURITY RISKS AND COUNTERTERRORISM CHALLENGES, November 2015, Preliminary Findings of a House Homeland Security Committee Review ,https://homeland.house.gov/wp-content/uploads/2015/11/HomelandSecurityCommittee_Syrian_Refugee_Report.pdf,pp.2-3.Electronically accessed 21 March 2016, 7 p.m. IST.
68. Robert S. Leiken, "http://www.cfr.org/religion/europes-angry-muslims/p8218",Foreign Affairs, July/August 2005. Electronically accessed on 26 July 2016, 10 pm IST.
69. [U.S. House of Representatives] Homeland Security Committee, FINAL REPORT OF THE TASK FORCE ON COMBATING TERRORIST AND FOREIGN FIGHTER TRAVEL, September 2015, .pdf, p. 6.
70. FINAL REPORT, September 2015, op.cit. pp .49, 50.
71. FINAL REPORT, September 2015, op.cit. p.50.
72. NYT, March 19, 2016, op.cit.
73. Video Polittalk, ZDF TV. "Feinde im eigenen Land...", op.cit. 22:15 | 31. März 2016
74. SYRIAN REFUGEE FLOWS..., November 2015, op.cit.
75. VIDEO,http://www.spiegel.de/sptv/magazin/,29.02.2016, electronically accessed pn 18 March 2016. 3.50 IST.

76. Http://www.bbc.com/news/world-africa-35346332, 18 January 2016. Electronically accessed on 3/22/2016 , 7:56 PM IST; The Telegraph, Kolkata, 26 March 2016.
77. DAVID A. GRAHAM, "French authorities say they believe Abdelhamid Abaaoud, a 27-year-old Belgian man, masterminded the November 13 attacks in Paris", www.theatlantic.com/international/archive/2015/11/...islam.../416235/ The Atlantic, NOV 17,2015 Electronically accessed on 4 April 2016, 7:42 PM IST.
78. Ishaan Tharoor,"Belgium's big problem with radical Islam", quoting BuzzFeed's Joshua Hersh. Https://www.washingtonpost.com/news/worldviews/wp/2016/03/22/belgiums-big-problem-with-radical-islam/, March 22, 2016. Electronically accessed on 21 May 2016, 9.00pm IST.
79. Molenbeek is a small suburb of Brussels. Maelbeek or Maalbeek is the metro station just two miles away. Http://www.independent.co.uk/news/world/europe/brussels-attacks-a-look-at-molenbeek-the-small-belgian-suburb-home-to-some-of-the-world-s-most-a6946321.html,22 March 2016. Electronically accessed on 05 April 2016, 7.55 am, IST.
80. Patrick Knox, "Molenbeek UNMASKED: Inside Europe's Jihadi capital where ISIS hatched worst terror attacks", http://www.dailystar.co.uk/news/latest-news/515259/Molenbeek-muslim-Brussels-attacks-Belgium-Paris-Thales-ISIS-jihad-jihadi-HQ, 15th May 2016. Electronically accessed on 05 July 2016, 9.00 pm IST.
81. In other ways, however, Molenbeek is said to be rather different. It has a strong middle class, bustling commercial districts, and a gentrifying artist class. Graham, op.cit. Secunder Kermani,"Molenbeek's gangster jihadists", http://www.bbc.com/news/magazine-35890960, 24 March 2016. Electronically accessed on 10 April 2016, 2.23 am IST.
82. According to a BBC report, approximately half of Molenbeek's population are of Muslim descent and in some parts even 70-80%. Around a third of its population was unemployed as of 2012 (BBC chart). "I notice that each time there is a link with Molenbeek," Belgian Prime Minister Charles Michel said, "This is a gigantic problem. Apart from prevention, we should also focus more on repression." (That unfortunate wording may be a failure of translation. [The Atlantic]) Interior Minister Jan Jambon added: "We don't have control of the situation in Molenbeek at present." Jambon's statement has reawakened concerns about Muslim "no-go zones" in European cities. "According to the myth", comments The Atlantic, " there were large zones that police forces had simply ceded to sharia gangs, and into which neither non-Muslims nor law enforcement dared to go." DAVID A. GRAHAM, "What's the Matter With Belgium?" NOV 17, 2015,http://www.theatlantic.com/international/archive/2015/11/belgium-radical-islam-jihad-molenbeek-IS/416235/, NOV 17, 2016. Electronically accessed on 23 March 2016, 4.45 pm IST; Alex Forsyth, Paris attacks: Is Molenbeek a haven for Belgian jihadis? http://www.bbc.com/news/world-europe-34839403,17 November 2015. Electronically accessed on 23 March 2016, 5.09 pm IST.

83. "Hooligans stören Trauerfeier in Brüssel", http://www.handelsblatt.com/politik/international/nach-den-anschlaegen-hooligans-stoeren-trauerfeier-in-bruessel/13370868.html?nlayer=News_1985586, 27.03.2016 16:00 CET
84. Greg Botelho, Paul Cruickshank and Michael Pearson, "Paris attackers linked in Morocco arrest", http://edition.cnn.com/2016/03/18/world/paris-attack-salah-abdeslam-fingerprints-capture/,0041 GMT, March 19, 2016; TV channels Al-Jazeera, BBC, CNN, India Today, Times Now, NewsX, 22, 23 March 2016, 1.30-2.40 pm IST. "Brussels attacks: Zaventem and Maelbeek bombs kill many", http://www.bbc.com/news/world-europe-35869254, 22 March 2016. Electronically accessed on 23 March 2016, 4.15 pm IST. The Telegraph, Kolkata, 23 March 2016. Two of the suicide bombers who carried out attacks in Brussels on 22 March 2016 have been named as brothers Khalid and Brahim el-Bakraoui, Belgian nationals. Brahim was part of the attack at Zaventem airport that killed 11 people. Khalid struck at Maelbeek metro, where 20 people died. "Brussels attacks: Two brothers behind Belgium bombings. Two other attackers at the airport have not yet been identified. One of them died, another is on the run."Http://www.bbc.com/news/world-europe-35879141, 23 March 2016, 9.50 pm IST. One of the two suicide bombers at Brussels airport was also involved in the November 2015 Paris attacks. Najim Lachraoui, 24, was a Belgian citizen and, as mentioned earlier, had visited Syria in February 2013. He was a bomb maker. As of 25 March 2016 nine suspects were arrested in Belgium and Germany in a widening swoop also across France, Spain and the Netherlands. BBC TV, 26 March 2016, 1.30 pm and The Telegraph, Kolkata, 26 March 2016.
85. CNN TV, 22 March 2016, 1.40 pm IST; "Brussels attacks…", op.cit.
86. Seth G. Jones, "The Terrorism Threat to the United States and Implications for Refugees", RAND CT-433, June 2015,Testimony presented before the House Homeland Security Committee, Subcommittee on Counterterrorism and Intelligence on June 24, 2015,.pdf, p. 4.
87. The citation was to Hanumanth Ramesh and Veryan Khan, "TRAC Insight: Refugees Organised Crime's New Market and Jihadis' New Cover," TRAC Insight, September 15, 2015, http://www.trackingterrorism.org/chatter/trac-insight-syrianrefugees-organised-crimes-new-market-and-jihadis-newcover. According to defector Abu Khaled, the secretive Amn al-Kharji, responsible for conducting espionage and terrorist attacks in enemy territory, is one of four agencies that fall under IS's amniyat, or security apparatus. According to a study,the structure of IS's Amn al-Kharji and the group's tactics in the Paris and Brussels attacks make immediately clear that IS has fully professionalised its external operations. IS militants operating in Europe are well-trained and are commanded by veteran jihadists with years of experience. IS's activities in Europe are more akin to those of a state sponsor of terrorism than to those of a non-state actor. Daveed Gartenstein-Ross, Nathaniel Barr, "[Hot Issue] Recent Attacks Illuminate

the Islamic State's Europe Attack Network", http://www.jamestown.org/single/?tx_ttnews%5Btt_news%5D=45362&tx_ttnews%5BbackPid%5D=7&cHash=480fc6c02c16ce0b3571fc5635fd699c#.VyOFb9R95kg. April 27, 2016 03:12 PM ET.

88. SYRIAN REFUGEE FLOWS..., November 2015, op.cit. p. 6.
89. NYT, March 19, 2016, op.cit.
90. Findings 6-10 of SYRIAN REFUGEE FLOWS... November 2015, op.cit. pp. 6-9.
91. "FBI Tipped Off Dutch Police One Week Before Brussels Attack", https://www.clarionproject.org/news/fbi-tipped-dutch-police-week-brussels-attack, March 31, 2016. Electronically accessed on 04 April 2016, 2.00 pm IST. The Islamic State jihadists had also collected information about the home of Belgian Prime Minister Charles Michel. Building plans and photos were found on a computer dumped in a rubbish bin, according to the BBC.
92. Bruno Waterfield et al., "Blunders let bombers slip through net", The Times, London, reprinted in The Telegraph, Kolkata, 25 March 2016.
93. Bruno Waterfield ", op.cit.
94. ELLIOT FRIEDLAND, "Police Claim 50 IS Sympathizers Worked at Brussels Airport , https://www.clarionproject.org/analysis/police-claim-50-IS-sympathizers-worked-brussels-airport, April 3, 2016, quoting the Daily Mail. Electronically accessed on 04 April 2016, 2.15 am IST.
95. ANTHONY JOSEPH, "'It was a complete failure': France admits intelligence disaster as it is revealed Turkey warned of Paris attack jihadis a YEAR ago", http://www.dailymail.co.uk/news/article-3330073/Turkey-warned-France-Belgium-Paris-terrorists-year-ago.html,23 November 2015, 13:16 GMT; "Turkey's Erdogan says Belgium should account for intelligence failures",http://www.thestar.com.my/news/world/2016/03/26/turkeys-erdogan-says-belgium-should-account-for-intelligence-failures/ 26 March 2016, MYT 12:18 AM.
96. SYRIAN REFUGEE FLOWS..., November 2015, op.cit., p.9. The other recommendations included an end-to-end review of the refugee screening and vetting process, implementation of the recommendations of the bipartisan Congressional Task Force on Combating Terrorist and Foreign Fighter Travel, concerted effort by U.S. intelligence and law-enforcement agencies with America's European partners to review all data already collected from refugees and migrantsand to screen it against counterterrorism and intelligence databases, US assistance to its European partners in building robust counterterrorism capacity, work with Europe and the Middle East to close information-sharing gaps and improve intelligence and law enforcement cooperation related to Syrian refugees and, of course, to roll back and defeat IS.
97. "Before the final shootout, four mysterious hours in San Bernardino", https://www.washingtonpost.com/world/national-security/before-the-final-shootout-four-mysterious-hours-in-san-bernardino/

2015/12/14/95dd65f4-a299-11e5-9c4e-be37f66848bb_story.html. Electronically accessed on 3/22/2016, 9:02 PM IST: "San Bernardino shooting: What we know so far", http://www.bbc.com/news/world-us-canada-34993344, 11 December 2015. Electronically accessed on 3/22/2016, 9:13 PM.

98. Dabiq, op. cit. Shahādah: the Muslim profession of faith ('there is no god but Allah, and Muhammad is the messenger of Allah'), one of the Five Pillars of Islam; mujāhid: is one who struggles for the sake of Allah and Islam; jihad: holy war; .taqwā: God-fearing piety; Khilāfah": a person who safeguards the foundation of Islam. http://www.islamweb.net/emainpage/index.php?page=showfatwa&Option=FatwaId&Id=87908. Electronically accessed on 04 April 2016, 8 pm IST.

99. Laura Quran, "CIA chief wants to strengthen refugee screening", http://edition.cnn.com/2015/11/18/politics/cia-chief-wants-to-strengthen-refugee-screening/, 2210 GMT (0610 HKT) November 18, 2015. Electronically accessed on 22 March 2016, 9.35 pm IST.

100. Seth G. Jones, op.cit.

101. Right-wing Parties in Europe include:

Law and Justice	Poland
Swiss People's Party	Switzerland
Danish People's Party	Denmark
Freedom Party of Austria	Austria
New Flemish Alliance	Belgium
Finns Party	Finland
Progress Party	Norway
National Front	France
Sweden Democrats	Sweden
Swedish Resistance Movement	Sweden
United Kingdom Independence Party	United Kingdom
Party for Freedom	Netherlands
Alternative for Germany	Germany
National Democratic Party	Germany

https://en.wikipedia.org/wiki/List_of_active_nationalist_parties_in_Europe Electronically accessed on April 8,2016, 9:36 PM IST.

102. The hatred comes in many forms. It is expressed on the streets and on the internet. There have been more than twice as many attacks on refugee hostels during the first nine months of 2015 as in the whole of 2014. The rising tide of hatred is now reaching the politicians many hold responsible for the perceived chaos besetting Germany. The national headquarters of Merkel's conservative Christian Democratic Union (CDU) party in Berlin fields thousands of hate mails every week. Alberto Nardelli,"Rightwing parties are on the rise but they won't win power without women",https://www.theguardian.com/news/datablog/2016/jan/26/rightwing-parties-are-on-the-rise-but-they-wont-win-power-without-women, 26 January 2016 13.44 GMT. "Populist, Pernicious and Perilous.

Germany's Growing Hate Problem",http://www.spiegel.de/international/germany/a-1059357-druck.html, October 23,2015 07:42 PM CET. See also "Fury and the AfD. The Revolt against Angela Merkel", http://www.spiegel.de/international/germany/success-of-afd-populists-akin-to-revolt-against-merkel-a-1083147.html,March 03,21/2016 03:27 PM CET; Ian Bremmer,"These 5 Facts Explain the Worrying Rise of Europe's Far-Right",http://time.com/4075396/far-right-politics-rise-europe/,Oct. 15, 2015 . Electronically accessed on March 27,2016, 3:21 AM IST.

103. TV editorial staff (Chief Editor Jürgen Elsaesser und his colleagues Martin Müller-Mertens and Marc Dassen), "COMPACT 4/2016: Merkel im Erdowahn", 31.March 2016, http://tv.compact-online.de/. Electronically accessed on 11 April 2016, 5.00 am IST.
104. See Nardelli, op. cit.
105. Angelique Chrisafis' report in The Guardian: Marine Le Pen, the leader of France's far-right Front National, has been acquitted of inciting hatred after she compared Muslim street prayers to the Nazi occupation, http://www.theguardian.com/world/2015/dec/15/marine-le-pen-not-guilty-inciting-religious-hatred-lyon-french-front-national, 15 December 2015 15.17 GMT.
106. Angelique Chrisafis, "French elections: Front National makes no gains in final round", http://www.theguardian.com/world/2015/dec/13/front-national-fails-to-win-control-of-target-regions-amid-tactical-voting,14 December 2015 07.21 GMT; "Why are anti-immigration parties so strong in the Nordic states?",http://www.theguardian.com/news/datablog/2015/jun/19/rightwing-anti-immigration-parties-nordic-countries-denmark-sweden-finland-norway, 19 June 2015 17.10 BST.
107. Even though the Finns party (PS) received actually less votes in the April 2015 elections (17.7%) compared to that in 2011 (21.1%), due to the Finnish electoral system the PS became the second largest party in terms of parliamentary seats. http://balticworlds.com/a-centre-right-government-takes-form-in-finland/," A CENTRE-RIGHT GOVERNMENT TAKES FORM IN FINLAND", May 12, 2015. Electronically accessed on 06 July 2016, 9.34 pm IST.
108. Chrisafis, op. cit.; "Why are anti-immigration parties...", op.cit.
109. "Right-Wing Extremism", http://www.spiegel.de/international/topic/right_wing_extremism/.Electronically accessed on April 8, 2016, 9:42 PM IST.
110. "Syrian refugees should be trained into an army to fight IS, Poland's foreign minister says", http://www.independent.co.uk/news/uk/politics/syrian-refugees-should-be-trained-into-an-army-to-fight-IS-polands-foreign-minister-says-a6736776.html, 16 November 2015. Electronically accessed on 02 January 2016, 10.00 pm IST; "Hungarian PM: We don't want more Muslims",http://www.aljazeera.com/news/2015/09/refugees-hungary-train-station-150903064140564.html, 04 Sep 2015 06:51 GMT.

111. Brandt & Kelinhubbert, op,.cit.
112. "German right-leaning AfD leader calls for police right to shoot at refugees", http://www.dw.com/en/german-right-leaning-afd-leader-calls-for-police-right-to-shoot-at-refugees/a-19013137; "Transcript: Tim Sebastian interviews Frauke Petry", http://www.dw.com/en/transcript-tim-sebastian-interviews-frauke-petry/a-19152089, Electronically accessed on 11 April 2016, 2.00 am IST.
113. "German right-leaning AfD leader...", op. cit. See also http://www.independent.co.uk/voices/rise-of-afd-is-about-more-than-the-refugee-crisisis-but-angela-merkel-is-no-more-secure-for-that-a6931376.html, 15 March 2016, for more on AfD. Electronically accessed on 02 May 2016, 7.00 am IST.
114. Video discussion: Angst vor der Parallelgesellschaft. Kann Deutschland Integration? http://www.zdf.de/maybrit-illner/angst-vor-der-parallelgesellschaft-kann-deutschland-integration-43180420.html, 22.04.2016, 10.14 pm CEt. Electronically accessed on 23 April 2016, 9.32 pm IST. The AfD opposes building of minarets, the prayer call of the muezzin and the Sharia which, says Gauland, are symbols of dominance. There is no separation of religion and state in Islam, unlike the fundament on which Western democracy is based.
115. "Bericht: AfD setzt künftig vermehrt auf Islamkritik",http://www.merkur.de/politik/afd-setzt-laut-spiegel-kuenftigem-parteiprogramm-islamkritik-zr-6204639.html. 12 March2016, 5:14 pm CET.
116. Severin Weiland and Melanie Amann, "AfD-Zusammenkunft in Stuttgart: Die gelenkte Partei",http://www.spiegel.de/politik/deutschland/afd-parteitag-die-zusammenfassung-der-wichtigsten-ereignisse-a-1090277.html, 01.05.2016 7:20 pm CET. See esp. Chapters 7 and 9, Programm fuer Deutschland.Grundstazprogramm der Alternative fuer Deutschland, Bundesparteitag, Stuttgart, 30 April-91 May 2016, .pdf file.
117. Melanie Amann, et al., "The Rise of Germany's New Right", op.cit.
118. "Geert Wilders on BBC Hardtalk," (2 parts, the citation is from Part 1, Published on Dec 3, 2012),https://www.youtube.com/watchv=cSe0HD6bzqY&nohtml5=False; and Book review, June 13, 2012,Geert Wilders, Marked for Death: Islam's War Against the West and Me, Regnery,2012,http://www.washingtontimes.com/news/2012/jun/13/how-free-speech-led-to-jihad/. Electronically accessed on 12 April 2016, 8.16 pm IST. Wilders never goes anywhere without his government-assigned security contingent. While he was in Rome to receive the Oriana Fallaci Free Speech Award in 2009, a colleague counted 35 policemen guarding the door when Mr. Wilders went to the restroom. He joked that it was "the best-protected pee" of his life!
119. Foreign Affairs essay published in 1993, which became a book, propounds the thesis that human beings are divided along cultural lines Western, Islamic, Hindu and so on. There is no universal civilization. Instead, there

are these cultural blocks, each within its own distinct set of values. The Islamic civilization, in his view, is the most problematic. The Arab world does not share the values and criteria of the Western world. Their primary attachment is to their religion, not to their nation-state. Their culture is inhospitable to certain liberal ideals, like pluralism, individualism and democracy. A critical discussion in David Brooks, "Huntington's Clash Revisited", http://www.nytimes.com/2011/03/04/opinion/04brooks.html?_r=0, March 3, 2011. Electronically accessed on 05 July 2016, 9 pm IST.

120. Cited in Soeren Kern, "Geert Wilders: 'Marked for Death: Islam's War against the West and Me'", http://www.gatestoneinstitute.org/3041/geert-wilders-marked-for-death, April 30, 2012 4:15 am.
121. Soeren Kern, "Geert Wilders...", op.cit.
122. Vivienne Walt,"Marine Le Pen",http://time.com/3823288/marine-le-pen-2015-time-100/,April 16, 2015. Electronically accessed on 13 April 2016, 8.25 pm IST.
123. "Marine Le Pen", https://en.wikipedia.org/wiki/Marine_Le_Pen. Electronically accessed on 13 April 2016, 8.40 pm IST.
124. Adam Nossiter, "Marine Le Pen's Anti-Islam Message Gains Influence in France", http://www.nytimes.com/2015/11/18/world/europe/marine-le-pens-anti-islam-message-gains-influence-in-france.html?_r=0, NOV. 17, 2015, Electronically accessed on 13 April 2016, 8.22 pm IST.
125. Report by IAN SPARKS, http://www.dailymail.co.uk/news/article-3353002/Calais-Right-wing-town-France-Marine-Le-Pen-s-National-score-massive-49-cent-votes-home-Jungle.html, 10 December 2015 , 00:56 GMT,
126. Refugees 'look like an army', says Hungarian PM Viktor Orban",Agence France Presse, http://www.theguardian.com/world/2015/oct/23/refugees-look-like-an-army-says-hungarian-pm-viktor-orban, 23 October 2015, 01.42 BST.
127. Rita Pálfi,"Hungary's prime minister suspects "masterplan" is behind refugee crisisis", http://www.euronews.com/2015/11/13/hungarian-prime-minister-talks-about-leftist-masterplan-behind-refugee-crisisis/ 13 November 2015, 17:25 CET.
128. Maximilian Popp and Andreas Wassermann, " Prying into Pegida: Where Did Germany's Islamophobes Come From?" http://www.spiegel.de/international/germany/origins-of-german-anti-muslim-group-pegida-a-1012522.html, January 12, 2015 05:38 PM CET.
129. "Populist, Pernicious and Perilous...", op.cit.
130. "Populist, Pernicious and Perilous...", op.cit.
131. "Right-Wing Extremism: Germany's New Islamophobia Boom", http://www.spiegel.de/international/germany/islamophobic-hate-groups-become-more-prominent-in-germany-a-956801.html, March 05, 2014 05:02 PM CET.
132. https://en.wikipedia.org/wiki/Akif_Pirin%C3%A7ci; http://www.dw.com/en/publisher-abandons-turkish-born-pirincci-

over-pegida-speech/a-18794193. Electronically accessed on 23 April 2016, 8.45 pm IST.

133. The Armenian Resolution determined that the Ottoman Empire, the predecessor of modern Turkey, did commit a "genocide" against the Armenians during 1915-16, which Ankara vehemently denies. Turkish-origin German citizen and Green Party leader Oezdemir reportedly took the initiative to introduce the rsolution. Berlin decided to enhance the security status of the threatened Turkish-origin MPs. "Nach Armenien-Resolution: Deutsch-türkische Abgeordnete bekommen mehr Polizeischutz",http://www.spiegel.de/politik/deutschland/armenien-deutsch-tuerkische-abgeordnete-erhalten-mehr-polizeischutz-a-1097118.html, 11 June 2016; „Ja, Völkermord", http://www.zeit.de/politik/deutschland/2016-06/armenien-resolution-voelkermord-joachim-gauck-die-gruenen, 1. Juni 2016.

134. Heinz Buschkowsky, Die andere Gesellschaft, Ullstein Buchverlage GmbH, Berlin, 2014, pp.9-10, 31. On Neukoelln see Moises Mendoza, "Neukölln Nasties: Foreigners Feel Accused in Berlin Gentrification Row",http://www.spiegel.de/international/germany/neukoelln-nasties-foreigners-feel-accused-in-berlin-gentrification-row-a-750297.html, March 11, 2011 04:31 PM.

135. Buschkowsky, op. cit. p. 43.

136. Buschkowsky, op. cit. pp. 60-61.

137. There were roughly four million Muslims living in Germany as of 2014. Buschkowsky, op. Cit.p.64. A Half to three-quarter million of them were Alewites, so not dogmatic Muslims. An estimated one-third of the Muslims could be considered dogmatic. There were an estimated 43,000 of these who belonged to the radical spectrum as of 2014, with 500 fighters from Syria and Iraq seen as "deadly danger". Bundesverfassungsbericht 2013, cited in Buschkowsky, op. Cit. p. 260.

138. Buschkowsky, op. Cit. pp. 264-265, 296,298.

139. "Wir brauchen Antworten, die wehtun",interview with Christoph Heinemann, http://www.deutschlandfunk.de/heinz-buschkowsky-zu-vorfaellen-in-koeln-wir-brauchen.694.de.html?dram:article_id=341740, 7January.2016,07:20amCET. Electronically accessed on 14 April 2016, 2.30 am IST.

140. Thilo Sarrazin, Deutschland schafft sich ab, Wie wir unser Land aufs Spiel setzen, Deutsche Verlags-Anstalt, Muenchen, 13. ed., 2010.

141. "TIGHTEN YOUR SEAT BELTS: THILO SARRAZIN TO PUBLISH NEW BOOK",http://www.germerica.com/2016/04/20/thilo-sarrazin-coming-new-book/, APRIL 20, 2016. Electronically accessed on 22 April 2016, 10.37 am IST.

142. Sarrazin,, op.cit., pp.58-64. His interview with the Austrian newspaper, Kurier, is revealing. Here an excerpt: "KURIER: "I don't want the land of my grandchildren to be, in large parts, Islamic, ... the women wearing the veil and daily life being defined by the rhythms of the muezzin" - is it necessary to exaggerate so much to be heard?

Thilo Sarrazin: It's no exaggeration. That is the social reality in specific parts of Berlin. And it's materialising at high speed.
KURIER: Because of demographics?
Thilo Sarrazin: And continued immigration. You need to take a look at specific districts and see how things have changed there in the last 40 years. Güner Balci, an editor of Turkish origin, said recently in the *FAZ am Sonntag* [newspaper]: "20 years ago there was a colourful mixed society, then ever more people moved out. It became more aggressive. Violence increased on the streets. Ever more women and girls wore the veil. Another worldview established itself." This negative development is spreading further." Interview with Thilo Sarrazin", Posted by Cheradenine Zakalwe, 25 September 2011, http://islamversuseurope.blogspot.in/2011/09/interview-with-thilo-sarrazin.html. Electronically accessed on 22 April 2016, 10 30 am, IST.

143. Sarrazin, op.cit., pp.362-364.
144. CHRIS TOMLINSON,"Best Selling Author Slams Merkel's Migrant Policy in New Book",http://www.breitbart.com/london/2016/04/21/ex-senator-sarrazin-slams-merkels-migrant-policy-new-book/,21 Apr 2016. Electronically accessed on 22 April 2016, 11.00 am IST.
145. See, for instance, CDU political figure, Hamburg's former First Mayor and Chair, Atomic Commission, Ole von Beust, "Das Boese blossstellen", http://www.zeit.de/gesellschaft/2016-04/thilo-sarrazin-ole-von-beust-fluechtlinge-afd/komplettansicht. 1 May 2016, 3.02 pm CET.
146. Gabriel T. Sabarani, Jihad's New Heartlands: Wh the West Has Failed to Contain Islamic Fundamentalism, AuthorHouse, (UK), Milton Keynes, 2011, p. 294 (via books.google.com/); The American Foreign Policy Council, Almanac of Islamism, July 10, 2013, http://almanac.afpc.org/archive/50
147. Schulte-Peevers, Andrea; Haywood, Anthony; Johnstone, Sarah; Gray, Jeremy; Daniel, Robinson (2007), Germany, Lonely Planet, ISBN 1-74059-988-8. Turks constitute 63.2% of all Muslims in Germany, immigrants from the Mid-East and North Africa make up 15%, from Southeast Europe 13.6%. Charles Hawley, Victory for Intolerance: How Islamophobes Launched a National Debate, http://www.spiegel.de/international/germany/recent-german-debate-on-islam-triggered-by-tiny-anti-muslim-party-a-836527.html, June 01, 2012.
148. "Islam in Germany", http://www.euro-islam.info/country-profiles/germany/. Electronically accessed on 15 April 2016, 1.00 am IST.
149. Dr.Hans-Peter Friedrich, Federal Minister and Member of Parliament, BfV Report 2012, p. 232; American Foreign Policy Council, Almanac of Islamism, July 10, 2013, http://almanac.afpc.org/archive/50
150. Pénélope Larzillère, "Palästinensische Studenten in Deutschland und Frankreich", in: Alexandre Escudier et al.(eds), Der Islam in Europa: Der Umgang mit dem Islam in Frankreich und Deutschland, Berlin-Brandenburgischen Institut für Deutsch-Französische Zusammenarbeit in Europa, vol. 05, Wallstein Verlag,Göttingen, 2003, pp.107-120, cited in "Islam in Germany", op.cit.

151. Sabarani, ibid., p.293. See also http://www.euro-islam.info/2014/11/05/number-muslims-france-largely-overestimated/
152. "Germany: Extremism and Counter-Extremism", http://www.counterextremism.com/countries/germany. Electronically accessed on 13 July 2016, 9.23 pm IST.
153. "IS zeigt Video des Attentäters und übernimmt Verantwortung für den Zug-Angriff", Yahoo Nachrichten, https://de.nachrichten.yahoo.com/is-%C3%BCbernimmt-verantwortung-f%C3%BCr-zug-angriff-084901661.html, 19. Juli 2016.
154. "Bombenanschlag platzt in Beamtenstadt-Idylle", https://de.nachrichten.yahoo.com/bombenanschlag-platzt-in-beamtenstadt-idylle-054401024.html, Yahoo Nachrichten, 25 July 2016; Anton Troianovski, Todd Buell, "Ansbach Bombing in Germany Believed to Be Islamist Terror Attack",http://www.wsj.com/articles/syrian-asylum-seeker-blows-himself-up-outside-concert-in-germany-1469447416, July 25, 2016 1:20 p.m. ET; Daleel had pledged allegiance to Islamic State in a video announcing his intention to murder Germans "because they help kill Muslims". "Backpack bomber left film pledging allegiance to Isis", http://www.thetimes.co.uk/edition/world/backpack-bomber-signed-up-to-isis-before-targeting-germans-fxmrd8rj6, July 26 2016, 12:01 am, [UTC].
155. See, for instance, "Kopftuchverbot: Berliner Lehrerin mit Klage gescheitert", http://www.focus.de/politik/deutschland/fuehlte-sich-diskriminiert-berliner-lehrerin-mit-klage-gegen-kopftuchverbot-gescheitert_id_5437222.html, 14.04.2016, 6:12 pm CET; „TU Berlin Die Universität als Moschee?"http://www.faz.net/aktuell/feuilleton/tu-berlin-die-universitaet-als-moschee-14122316.html,14.03.2016, 2:59 pm CET.
156. Federal Ministry of the Interior, 2014 ANNUAL REPORT ON THE PROTECTION OF THE CONSTITUTION: FACTS AND TRENDS, www.verfassungsschutz.de, pdf file, p.23. Electronically accessed on April 2016, 9.00 pm IST.
157. "What is Islamism?" Bundesamt für Verfassungsschutz, https://www.verfassungsschutz.de/en/fields-of-work/islamism-and-islamist-terrorism/what-is-islamism. Electronically accessed on April 16,2016, 8:45 PM IST.
158. Foreword by Dr.Hans-Peter Firedrich, Federal Minister and Member of Parliament, 2nd. Paragraph, Bundesverfassungsschutzbericht 2012; and BfV Report 2013, p.28, Berlin; BfV Report 2013, Fakten und Tendenzen, Kurzzusammenfassung, Berlin, p. 21, http://www.verfassungsschutz.de.
159. Salim Mansur,Islam and Islamism,http://www.gatestoneinstitute.org/3865/islam-islamism, July 23, 2013; BfV Report 2013, op.cit.
160. FALIH HASSAN, TIM ARANGO And OMAR AL-JAWOSHY, "Bombing kills more than 140 in Baghdad"
161. Claudia Luzar, Researcher of Conflict and Right-wing Extremism citing a Univ. of Bielefeld study, on TV programme "Hooligans gegen Salafisten -

Straßenkampf in Deutschland" - phoenix Runde of 29.10.2014,https://www.youtube.com/watch?v=5ChrSNvVG14&list=PLoeytWjTuSurss7bwyGAhXbPU9684JphA. A growing number of Islamic institutions in Germany is publicly calling the Muslim faithful to prayerfive times a day, seven days a weekwith cries of Allahu Akbar! ("Allah is Greater!" sic!)The sonorous prayer calls (known in Arabic as adhan) can be heard from great distances when amplified through electric loudspeakers. Soeren Kern, The Islamization of Germany in 2013, http://www.gatestoneinstitute.org/4130/islamization-germany, January 15, 2014.

162. BfV-Newsletter Nr. 2/2014, www.verfassungsschutz.de. Electronically accessed on 24 March 2016, 9.20 pm IST.
163. 2015AnalyseRadikalisierungsgruendeSyrienIrakAusreisende.pdf,, www.bka.de/, p.48. Electronically accessed on april 2, 2016, 10.pm IST.
164. BfV Report 2013, op.cit., pp.59-60, Salafismus. Dirk Baehr sees three types of Salafism, the purist (merely preaching), political (calling for political action beyond preaching) and jihadist (opting for violence). Baehr, op. cit.
165. Deutschlandfunk radio Mediathek, "Wie gross ist die Terrorgefahr durch Islamisten bzw.Salafisten?" Interview with author Ahmad Mansur, 10 February 2016, 12.30 pm CET. Electronically accessed on 14 April 2016, 5.30 am IST. According to Mansur, who wrote a vehement critique of the Salafists in his book Die Generation Allah, had long research experience and heads a violence-prevention agency in Berlin-Neukoelln, every third Salafist in Berlin is violence-prone while the pan-German average is every eighth. On BfV on jihad, "He is of the opinion that 1,800 people are ready to go from Germany and fight in Syria. His figure is higher than official estimates. Around 10,000 Salafists prepare these fighters while another 10,000 support the Salafist scene.
166. Foreword by Dr.Hans-Peter Friedrich, op.cit..; and BfV Report 2013, p.28, Berlin; BfV Report 2013, Fakten und Tendenzen, Kurzzusammenfassung, Berlin, p. 21, http://www.verfassungsschutz.de
167. Federal Ministry of the Interior, 2014 ANNUAL REPORT, op.cit. pp. 21-23,
168. Syrien und der unterschätzte Salafismus, http://www.inforadio.de/programm/schema/sendungen/zwoelfzweiundzwanzig/201410/211701.html , 25.10.2014 | 12:21 Central European Time, Zwölfzweiundzwanzig (radio interview of Dr. Hans-Georg Maassen).
169. "Germany: New Anti-Terrorism Legislation Entered Into Force", http://www.loc.gov/law/foreign-news/article/germany-new-anti-terrorism-legislation-entered-into-force/, July 10, 2015. Electronically accessed on 22 July 2016, 7.50 pm IST.
170. Federal Ministry of the Interior,2014 ANNUAL REPORT, op.cit. pp. 22-23.
171. The Telegraph, Kolkata, 3 Nov.2014, pp. 1, 4.
172. Interview of Dr. Maaßen: „Unser Geschäft lebt auch vom Verrat" in Handelsblatt No. 020, 29.01.2014, p.4, reproduced in www.verfassungsschutz.de, BfV-Newsletter Nr. 2/2014. At least 15 of the jihadists from Germany were killed. Regierung will EU-weite

Fluggastdatenspeicherung, http://www.zeit.de/politik/ausland/2014-10/islamischer-staat-terrorbekaempfung-fluggastdatenspeicherung-europaeische-union. 29. October 2014.

173. Maassen, ibid.; BND report in Islamisten: BND warnt vor IS-Anschlag im Westen, http://www.spiegel.de/politik/deutschland/bnd-warnt-vor-groesserem-is-anschlag-im-westen-a-1001835.html#ref=rss, 09.11.2014; https://www.verfassungsschutz.de/en/fields-of-work/islamism-and-islamist-terrorism/figures-and-facts-islamism/islamist-following-2014. Electronically accessed on April 16,2016, 8:42 PM IST.

174. Kern, op.cit.

175. BfV, Focal Topics..., op.cit.

176. BfV, Focal Topics..., op.cit.

177. BfV Report 2012, p.232; https://www.verfassungsschutz.de/en/fields-of-work/islamism-and-islamist-terrorism/figures-and-facts-islamism/islamist-following-2014. Electronically accessed on April 16,2016, 8:42 PM IST.

178. EU Terrorism Situation and Trend Report (TE-SAT) 2014, https://www.europol.europa.eu/sites/default/files/publications/europol_tsat14_web_1.pdf

179. Soeren Kern, "Salafi-Jihadists: "A Persistent Threat" to Europe and America",http://gatestmeininstitute.org/4355/salafi-jihadists-threat,%2013%20June%202014, and "Muslim Voters Change Europe", http://www.gatestoneinstitute.org/3064/muslim-voters-europe.

180. Verfasungsschutzbericht Niedersachsen 2013. Despite its regional focus, the report provides a wealth of information about the rise of radical Islam in Germany as a whole. The state of Lower Saxony houses a sizeable Muslim population (6.2%. The south German state of Baden-Wuerttemberg and Bavaria together accounts for 16.6%, the other southern state of Bavaria 13.2%. While Hesse has 10.3% and capital Berlin 6.9%, the western state of North Rhine-Westfalen alone accounts for 33.1%. Table Six: Regional distribution of Muslims in Germany, ECKHARD JESSE AND TOM MANNEWITZ, Impact of Counter-Terrorism on Communities: Germany Background Report, Instt. for Strategic Dialogue, Open Society Foundations,p.3, http://www.strategicdialogue.org/Country_Report_Germany_FW.pdf, p.11). Http://www.verfassungsschutz.niedersachsen.de/portal/live.php?navigation_id=12260&article_id=124756&_psmand=30.

181. BfV Report 2013, Fakten und Tendenzen, Kurzzusammenfassung, Berlin, p. 21, http://www.verfassungsschutz.de

182. Rashid, op. cit.

183. Soeren Kern, Germany: "Radical Salafism is Like a Hard Drug", http://www.gatestoneinstitute.org/3121/germany-radical-salafism, June 19, 2012.

184. Andrea Brandt and Guido Kleinhubbert, "New Front for the German Far Right: Anti-Islamic Party Is Playing With Fear",http://www.spiegel.de/international/germany/new-front-for-the-german-far-right-anti-

islamic-party-is-playing-with-fear-a-526225.html, January 03, 2008 04:32 pm CET. The PRO NRW was Germany's first anti-Islamist party.

185. BfV Report 2012, p.269. www.verfassungsschutz-berlin.de
186. BfV Report 2012, ibid.
187. BfV Report 2010, p.203. The youths, "self-radicalised"thanks to the internet, are difficult to identify and control. "Die Berliner Grspraeche. Djihad, error und Martyrtum" (Swiss Embassy),Audio: srv.deutschlandradio.de Fazit, 26.1.14, 03.15.
188. In a case that is revealing, an accidental explosion in a madrassa in a Burdwan village has led to central government investigations that continue to unravel far-reaching cross-border network of Islamist terrorism. The banned Jamaat-ul-Mujahideen Bangladesh (JMB) reportedly spread its tentacles in West Bengal, Assam and elsewhere to make bombs in India meant for use in Bangladesh. Indoctrination in Islamism was also being carried out simulaneously. The Telegraph, Kolkata, 16 October 2014, ABP Ananda TV, 26 Oct.2014, 1.00 pm.
189. www.verfassungsschutz.de,, Focal topics…, op.cit.
190. Frankfurter Flughafen-Attentäter bekommt lebenslänglich, http://www.zeit.de/gesellschaft/zeitgeschehen/2012-02/anschlag-frankfurt-flughafen-urteil, 10. Februar 2012. BfV Report 2013, p.44. See also Dorothea Jung, Tuerkische Vaeter und die Angst vor dem Djihad, AUDIO, 20.12.13, 22:10http://srv.deutschlandradio.de/themes/dradio/script/aod/index.html?audioMode=2&audioID=4.
191. Jörg Diehl, Messerattacke auf Bundespolizist: Angriff aus dem Nichts, http://www.spiegel.de/panorama/justiz/hannover-ermittler-fuerchten-nach-messerattacke-nachahmungstaeter-a-1080725.html.
192. Bundesamt für Verfassungsschutz, The Islamic State (IS) Threat to Germany? www.verfassungsschutz.de.
193. Federal Ministry of the Interior, 2014 ANNUAL REPORT, op.cit. p. 21.
194. Mark Owen, No Easy Day, Penguin, London, 2012, p.293. He goes on to observe: Osama bin Laden had not prepared to defend himself, though apparently he had plenty of time and an AK-47 and a Makarov pistol were within his reach. "He had no intention of fighting. He asked his followers for decades to wear suicide vests or fly planes into buildings, but didn't even pick up his weapon. In all my deployments, we routinely saw this phenomenon. The higher up the food chain the targeted individual was, the bigger a pussy he was. The leaders were less willing to fight. It is always the young and impressionable who strap on the explosives and blow themselves up." pp. 248-9.
195. BfV Report 2012, p.240. Radical extremists, including IS cells, are active also in India, Pakistan and Bangladesh. The accidental blast of explosives in Khagragarh locality of Burdwan district in West Bengal on 2 October 2014 followed by suicide bombing at the Indo-Pakistani border crossing point in Wagah a month later were among the pointers in this direction.
196. In 2010 Milli Goerues had over 300,000 members and perhaps another 100,000 sympathisers. It has a history of striving to establish an Islamic

state and society in Turkey. The Bundesverfassungsschutz has declared it as "foreign terrorist organisation". Sabarani, op.cit., p. 318.

197. BfV Report 2012, p. 204.
198. Gallup poll data reported from 2011, http://www.gallup.com/poll/157082/islamophobia-understanding-anti-muslim-sentiment-west.aspx. Electronically accessed on 14 April 2016, 9.00 pm IST.
199. Mark Townsend,: "Anti-Muslim prejudice 'is moving to the mainstream'", http://www.theguardian.com/world/2015/dec/05/far-right-muslim-cultural-civil-war, 5 December 2015 12.16 GMT.
200. "Right-Wing Extremism: Germany's New Islamophobia Boom", http://www.spiegel.de/international/germany/islamophobic-hate-groups-become-more-prominent-in-germany-a-956801.html, MARCH 05, 2014 05:02 PM CET.
201. Tom Engelhardt, " post-Paris "clash of civilizations"?" http://mondediplo.com/openpage/a-post-paris-clash-of-civilizations, NOVEMBER 2015. Electronically accessed on 10 April 2016, 7.55 pm IST.
202. "From Hypocrisy to Apostasy. The Extinction of the Grey Zone", Dabiq, Issue 7, (no Western date but 1436 Rabi'al-Akhir, pp.54-66, http://media.clarionproject.org/files/islamic-state/islamic-state-dabiq-magazine-issue-7-from-hypocrisy-to-apostasy.pdf. Electronically accessed on 12 March 2016, 7,30 pm IST.
203. "Gleiche Rechte und Pflichten für alle Ausländer", interview of de Maiziere by Antje Sirleschtov and Frank Jansen, Der Tagesspiegel / 03.04.2016, http://www.bmi.bund.de/SharedDocs/Interviews/DE/2016/03/interview-tagesspiegel.html. Electronically accessed on April 14, 2016, 9:03 PM IST.
204. "Von der heutigen Massnahme geht ein klares Signal aus", http://www.bmi.bund.de/SharedDocs/Pressemitteilungen/DE/2016/04/rueckfuehrung-einundzwanzig-georgier.html, Pressemitteilung 15.04.2016. Electronically accessed on 18 April 2016, 8.10 pm IST; "181.405 Asylantraege im ersten Quartal 2016", http://www.bmi.bund.de/SharedDocs/Pressemitteilungen/DE/2016/04/asylantraege-m%C3%A4rz-2016.html?nn=3315850, Pressemitteilung 08.04.2016. Electronically accessed on 18 April 2016, 8.12 pm IST.
205. "Integrationspflicht wird Gesetz', https://www.cdu.de/artikel/integrationspflicht-wird-gesetz,14.04.2016; "Germany moves towards new integration law for migrants", http://www.bbc.com/news/world-europe-36048397. Electronically accessed on April 15,2016, 12:53 AM IST.
206. CHRIS TOMLINSON,"The Turkish community in Berlin has rejected out of hand plans by the German government to forcibly integrate Muslims.",http://www.breitbart.com/london/2016/04/15/turkish-community-outraged-german-integration-scheme/, 15 Apr 2016. Electronically accessed on 22 April 2016, 11.12 am IST.
207. "Gleiche Rechte und Pflichten... ", op.cit.
208. Soeren Kern, ibid.
209. BfV Report 2012, pp. 230-1; Soeren Kern, ibid.

210. TE-SAT 2014, ibid. In May 2012 the PRO NRW had organised a caricature contest shaming Islam that provoked violent clashes with Salafists. Charles Hawley, op.cit.
211. TE-SAT 2014,EUROPEAN UNION TERRORISM SITUATION AND TREND REPORT 2014, https://www.europol.europa.eu/sites/default/files/publications/europol_tsat14_web_1.pdf
212. TE-SAT 2014, ibid.
213. Regierung will EU-weite Fluggastdatenspeicherung,, op.cit. Http://www.zeit.de/politik/ausland/2014-10/islamischer-staat-terrorbekaempfung-fluggastdatenspeicherung-europaeische-union. 29. Oktober 2014; Syrien und der unterschätzte Salafismus, http://www.inforadio.de/programm/schema/sendungen/zwoelfzweiundzwanzig/201410/211701.html , 25.10.2014 | 12:21 Central European Time, Zwölfzweiundzwanzig (radio interview of Dr. Maassen).
214. Die Exremismus-Falle, https://magazin.spiegel.de/digital/?utm_source=spon&utm_campaign=inhaltsverzeichnis#SP/2014/42/129736965, Der Spiegel, 42/2014.
215. Thilo Sarrazin's controversial yet popular book on the negative Muslim impact on Germany, Deutschland schafft sich ab ("Germany Does Itself In", DVA, Munich, 2010) is one among many pointers to growing resentment throughout Europe against Islamism.See http://de.wikipedia.org/wiki/Deutschland_schafft_sich_ab#.E2.80.9EZuwanderung_und_Integration.E2.80.9C. His Dutch counterpart is Islamophobe MP Geert Wilders.
The Man Who Divided Germany: Why Sarrazin's Integration Demagoguery Has Many Followers, http://www.spiegel.de/international/germany/the-man-who-divided-germany-why-sarrazin-s-integration-demagoguery-has-many-followers-a-715876.html, September 06, 2010.
216. Nachrichten. Bundeswehr-journal.de, 15 February 2015, http://www.bundeswehr-journal.de/2015/eines-der-schaerfsten-terrorismus-strafgesetze-europa/#more-4778, .pdf, pp. 1-3.
217. Soeren Kern, Muslim Voters Change Europe, http://www.gatestoneinstitute.org/3064/muslim-voters-europe, May 17, 2012. Hollande's government, however, lost the 2014 elections. Muslim voters, strangely enough, mostly voted for rival FN of Marine Le Pen. Colin Randall, "France's Muslims drawn to far right anti-immigration party", http://www.thenational.ae/world/europe/frances-muslims-drawn-to-far-right-anti-immigration-party#page2, April 1, 2014 .
218. Soeren Kern, Germany: Islam Becomes Campaign Issue, http://www.gatestoneinstitute.org/3666/germany-islam-elections,April 11, 2013; Soeren Kern, The Islamization of Germany in 2013, op. cit.
219. Johanna Mikl-Leitner, Federal Interior Minister, Verfassungsschutzbericht 2011, Bundesamt fuer Verfassungsschutz und Terrorbekaempfung, http://www.bmi.gv.at/cms/BMI_Verfassungsschutz/BVT_VSB_2011_online.pdf. See also Al Qaeda opens new training camp in Yemen - The Long ...

www.longwarjournal.org/archives/2009/11/al_qaeda_opens_new_t.php;Terrorism Havens: Somalia - Council on Foreign Relations, www.cfr.org › Somalia; Al-Qaida / Al-Qaeda (The Base) - GlobalSecurity.org, www.globalsecurity.org › ... › World › Para-military Groups › Islamic; Al Qaeda - Background - Al Qaeda | Inside The Terror ... PBS,www.pbs.org/wgbh/pages/frontline/shows/network/.../indictment.html

220. Committee on Experts on Terrorism (CODEXTER), Profiles on Counter-Terrorist Capacity. Germany, Nov.2011, www.coe.int/terrorism.pdf.
221. Transnational Terrorism..., op.cit., p. 7-12.
222. Transnational Terrorism..., ibid., pp. 13-14.
223. Transnational Terrorism..., ibid., pp. 19-20.
224. ECKHARD JESSE..., op.cit., p. 2.
225. "German justice minister: some 200 Germans probed in connection with Syria", http://www.dw.com/en/german-justice-minister-some-200-germans-probed-in-connection-with-syria/a-18903442, 09.12.2015. Electronically accessed on April16,2016, 8:51 pm IST.
226. "Koalitionsausschuss am 13. April 2016.Handlungsbedarf Terrorismusbekaempfung. Massnahmenkatalog", 13 April 2016. 160414-massnahmen-terrorismus.pdf. Electronically accessed on April12, 2016, 8:40 pm IST.
227. Gesetzentwurf: Kabinett beschließt neues Anti-Terror-Paket, http://www.spiegel.de/politik/deutschland/bundesregierung-beschliesst-anti-terror-paket-a-1095223.html, 01 June 2016.
228. BKA warnt vor Anschlag eines Deutschen in Kabul, http://www.faz.net/aktuell/politik/ausland/terrorismus-bka-warnt-vor-anschlag-eines-deutschen-in-kabul-13259215.html, 10.11.2014; GSG 9 der Bundespolizei, http://www.bundespolizei.de/DE/06Die-Bundespolizei/Organisation/BPOLP/GSG9/gsg9_node.html

    Transnational Terrorism, Security and the Rule of Law, Case Study: Germany, 20 Nov.2008,www.transnationalterrorism.eu/publications, php, WP 6, Deliverable 12b. The two departments are the Department of Activities (threatening security and extremist efforts of foreign nationals) and the Department of Islamist Extremists and Islamist Terrorism. See p.7, fn.14; Besuch der Bundeskanzlerin beim Verfassungsschutz: Angela Merkel würdigt die Arbeit des BfV

    http://www.verfassungsschutz.de/de/aktuelles/meldungen/me-20141031-bundeskanzlerin-besuchte-bfv?pk_campaign=RSS-Feed
229. BfV Report 2013, pp.28-9. Islamismus.www.verfassungsschutz-berlin.de.
230. Zerrbilder von Islam und Demokratie von Islam und Demokratie, Dr. Ehrhart Körting, Senator, Senatsverwaltung für Inneres und Sport, http://www.berlin.de/sen/inneres/verfassungsschutz/publikationen/im-fokus/, Februar 2011(henceforth, Zerrbilder).
231. Interview of Dr. Hans-Georg Maassen, in "Interview Dr. Maaßen: „Unser Geschäft lebt auch vom Verrat"", in Handelsblatt No. 020, 29.01.2014, p.4, reproduced in www.verfassungsschutz.de, BfV-Newsletter Nr. 2/2014. Electronically accessed on January 12,2015, 8:47 pm IST.

232. 2014 Annual Report on the Protection of the Constitution. Facts and Trends, https://www.verfassungsschutz.de/en/public-relations/publications/annual-reports.Electronically accessed on April 19.2015, 8:30 pm IST.

233. Http://www.bnd.bund.de/EN/Scope_of_Work/Coordination/Coordination_node.html;http://www.kommando.streitkraeftebasis.de/portal/a/kdoskb/ut/p/c4/04_SB8K8xLLM9MSSzPy8xBz9CP3I5EyrpHK94uykOyUfL3y1MySlOKS4hK93MQUvdLUpNSi0rxi_YJsR0UAUKJtgw!!/;http://www.bnd.bund.de/EN/Scope_of_Work/Offices/Offices_node.html. Electronically accessed on April22,2016, 8:45 pm IST.

234. "BND-Chef muss gehen: Spekulationen über Schindlers Demission", http://www.spiegel.de/politik/deutschland/gerhard-schindler-spekulationen-ueber-schindlers-demission-a-1089484.html, 27.04.2016 11:02 CET; Norbert Wallet, „Spann Wolfgang Schaeuble die Faeden?"http://www.stuttgarter-zeitung.de/inhalt.wechsel-an-der-bnd-spitze-spann-wolfgang-schaeuble-die-faeden.add2a9dc-75f6-4768-bfd0-680595543eb4.html, 27. April 2016 - 7:28 pm CET.

235. BND report in "Islamisten: BND warnt vor IS-Anschlag im Westen", http://www.spiegel.de/politik/deutschland/bnd-warnt-vor-groesserem-is-anschlag-im-westen-a-1001835.html#ref=rss, 09.11.2014. Electronically accessed on February 19.2015, 8:32 pm IST.

236. Andrea Thomas, "Germany's BND Criticizes Saudi Arabia's Role in Arab World",http://www.wsj.com/articles/germanys-bnd-criticizes-saudi-arabias-role-in-arab-world-1449079412, Dec. 2, 2015 1:03 p.m. ET; "'Time of looking away over': Germany warns Saudi Arabia to stop funding radical Islamists", https://www.rt.com/news/324936-germany-criticizes-saudi-arabia/,7 Dec, 2015 01:58 MSK; http://www.dailymail.co.uk/news/article-3242354/Saudi-offer-build-200-mosques-Germany-Syrian-migrants-slammed-cynical-Kingdom-not-offered-refugees-themselves.html, 29 April 2016. Electronically accessed on 29 April 2016, 5.00 am IST; Justin Huggler, "German vice-chancellor accuses Saudi Arabia of funding Islamic extremism in the West",http://www.telegraph.co.uk/news/worldnews/europe/germany/12035838/German-vice-chancellor-accuses-Saudi-Arabia-of-funding-Islamic-extremism-in-the-West.html. 2:16PM GMT, 06 Dec 2015.

237. Http://www.kommando.streitkraeftebasis.de/portal/a/kdoskb/!ut/p/c4/04_SB8K8xLLM9MSSzPy8xBz9CP3I5EyrpHK94uyk-OyUfL3y1MySlOKS4hK93MQU_YJsR0UABos3fg!!/. Electronically accessed on April 22.2016, 8:39 pm IST.

238. "Bundeskriminalamt",http://www.bka.de/nn_205924/DE/DasBKA/dasBka__node.html?__nnn=true;"The Bundeskriminalamt. The Profile" .pdf; https://en.wikipedia.org/wiki/Federal_Criminal_Police_Office_(Germany); "Our Mandate",http://www.bka.de/EN/TheBKA/OurMandate/ourMandate__node.html?__nnn=true. Electronically accessed 28 April 2016, 7.46 pm IST.

239. "Failed Train Attack: Second German Terror Suspect Arrested in Lebanon", http://www.spiegel.de/international/failed-train-attack-second-german-terror-suspect-arrested-in-lebanon-a-433382.html, August 24, 2006 01:29 PM CET.
240. "Gemeinsames Terrorismusabwehrzentrum (GTAZ Joint Counter-Terrorism Centre)", Bundesamt für Verfassungsschutz,https://www.verfassungsschutz.de/en/fields-of-work/islamism-and-islamist-terrorism/gtaz-en. Electronically accessed on April16,2016, 8:44 pm IST.
241. Besides Amt des Bundesverfassungsschutz(BfV) or the Federal Office for the Protection of he Constitution, these authorities include the criminal police, the secret service, customs, military intelligence, federal police, federal office for migrants and refugees, and 16 state-level criminal police entities as well as state offices of the BfV. Further, international cooperation is considered vital. BfV Report 2012, p.1119; http://www.bmi.bund.de/SharedDocs/Glossareintraege/DE/G/gatz_de.html?nn=109632.
242. Gemeinsames Terrorismusabwehrzentrum (GTAZ Joint Counter-Terrorism Centre), Bundesamt für Verfassungsschutz, http://www.verfassungsschutz.de/en/fields-of-work/islamism-and-islamist-terrorism/gtaz-en
243. De Maziere's speech, Phoenix TV, https://www.youtube.com/watch?v=dj0WFY6e6fo
244. http://www.bmi.bund.de/SharedDocs/Pressemitteilungen/DE/2016/01/charlie-hebdo-attentat-jahrestag.html. Electronically accessed on 24 April 2016, 8.17 pm IST.
245. "Refugee-Terrorists Arrested in Germany", http://newobserveronline.com/four-refugee-terrorists-arrested-in-germany/, FEBRUARY 4, 2016. Electronically accessed on March 9.2016, 8:34 pm IST.
246. The Telegraph; and TV channels like ABP Ananda and 24 Ghonta (1-2.30 pm newscasts), Kolkata, 03-27 Oct. 2014.
247. "THE REVIVAL OF JIHĀD IN BENGAL", Dabiq, Issue No.12, pp. 37-42; Madison Park et al., "Cafe attackers were Bangladeshi, authorities say",www.cnn.com/2016/07/02/asia/bangladesh-dhaka-shooting/, 2 July 2016, 6.37 pm GMT.
248. The Telegraph, Kolkata, 13 July 2016, p. 6.
249. "Gemeinsames Internetzentrum (GIZ Joint Internet Centre)", Bundesamt für Verfassungsschutz, https://www.verfassungsschutz.de/en/fields-of-work/islamism-and-islamist-terrorism/giz-en. Electronically accessed on April 16,2016, 8:40 pm IST.
250. ECKHARD JESSE..., op.cit., p.3; de Maiziere's speech, Berlin GTAZ convention, 28 Oct.2014, https://www.youtube.com/watch?v=dj0WFY6e6fo. In a number of countries, football hooliganism is associated with nationalist and far-right politics, often at a superficial level such as crude racism.
251. The Telegraph, Kolkata, 16 October 2014.

252. BfV Report 2013, Fakten und Tendenzen, Kurzzusammenfassung, Berlin, p. 21, http://www.verfassungsschutz.de; The Telegraph, Kolkata, 5 Nov.2014, p.2; Robert Hannigan,The web is a terrorist's command-and-control network of choice, http://www.ft.com/intl/cms/s/2/c89b6c58-6342-11e4-8a63-00144feabdc0.html#axzz3I7Jjs7jf, November 3, 2014; Sam Jones and Murad Ahmed in London,Tech groups aid terror, says UK spy chief, http://www.ft.com/intl/cms/s/2/4a35c0b2-636e-11e4-9a79-00144feabdc0.html#axzz3ICBd2ig5, November 3, 2014. GCHQ stands for Government Communications Headquarters.

253. Council of Europe, Reply to the Questionnaire on Special Investigation Techniques in Relation to Act of Terrorism, www.coe.int/t/dlapil/codexter/specinvestigation_EN.asp, .pdf, pages unnumbered.

254. ARD TV 6-minute video from MITTELDEUTSCHER RUNDFUNK" GSG 9 - der Kommandeur berichtet", GSG-9 Commander Olaf Lindner's interview, 22.02.2013, http://www.ardmediathek.de/tv/LexiTV/GSG-9-der-Kommandeur-berichtet/MDR-Fernsehen/Video?bcastId=7545188&documentId=11870850; "Mythos GSG 9", https://www.youtube.com/watch?v=HCSIdb0Wuzs, ZDF History, 23 Sept.2012. Electronically accessed on 04 April 2016, 10.30 pm IST. On these various units, Bundeswehr-journal.de, http://www.bundeswehr-journal.de/2012/40-jahre-kampf-dem-terror/#more-981, 2014, .pdf. Electronically accessed on 3 March 2016, 8.34 pm IST. "Terrorism in Germany",http://www.german-way.com/history-and-culture/germany/terrorism-in-germany/. Electronically accessed on 20 April 2016, 10 15 pm IST; "GSG 9", http://www.whodareswins.com/gsg-9-german-counter-terrorism-special-operations-unit.html. Electronically accessed on 20 April 2016, 10.04 pm, IST; https://en.wikipedia.org/wiki/Spezialeinsatzkommando, Electronically accessed on 21 April 2016, 6.10 pm, IST.

255. "MEK. Mobiles Einsatzkommando", http://sek-einsatz.de/spezialeinheiten/mek-mobiles-einsatzkommando/2275. Electronically accessed on 21 April 7.53 pm, IST.

256. "Germany's new anti-terror units: A paramilitary excess?", Interview of Professor Rafael Behr, a criminologist and sociology professor at the Hamburg police academy conducted by Volker Wagener, http://www.dw.com/en/germanys-new-anti-terror-units-a-paramilitary-excess/a-19010175.Electronically accessed on 21 April 6.50 pm, IST.

257. "Re: Difference between GSG-9 and KSK", http://sci.tech-archive.net/Archive/sci.military.moderated/2005-06/msg00016.html,Joachim Schmid,21 Jun 2005 03:59:15 +0200.Electronically accessed on 4 March 2016, 9.00 pm IST; Brandon Webb, "GERMANY'S KOMMANDO SPEZIALKRAFTE (KSK)",http://specialoperations.com/17520/germanys-kommando-spezialkrafte-ksk/,February 20, 2013. http://www.special-ops.org/4740/gsg-9-grenzschutzgruppe-9.html; http://www.dw.com/en/germanys-new-anti-terror-units-a-

paramilitary-excess/a-19010175. Electronically accessed on April 4,2016,10:39 pm IST.

258. "Kommando Spezialkraefte (KSK) German commandos EUROPE Jun 25, 2013 Eric SOF", http://www.special-ops.org/99/kommando-spezialkraefte-ksk-german-commandos.html. Electronically accessed on 18 April,2016,9.52 pm IST.

259. Sabrina Pabst, "Germany launches new anti-terror unit 'BFE+'", http://www.dw.com/en/germany-launches-new-anti-terror-unit-bfe/a-18923373. Electronically accessed on 21 April,2016,7.20 pm IST.

260. Pabst, op. cit.

261. Pabst, op. cit.

262. ECKHARD JESSE..., op.cit., p. 2.

263. "Japan zur Islamisierung Deutschands", report by Japanese journalist Sakai, www.youtube.com, March 23, 2015. Electronically accessed on 02 January 2016, 8.34 pm IST.

264. Video report, "Praevention gegen gewaltbereiten Salafismus", ARD TV,03 November 2014, 2.43 pm. Electronically accessed on 25 October 2015, 2.30 am IST.

265. Zerrbilder von Islam und Demokratie von Islam und Demokratie, Dr. Ehrhart Körting, Senator, Senatsverwaltung für Inneres und Sport, http://www.berlin.de/sen/inneres/verfassungsschutz/publikationen /im-fokus/, Februar 2011 (henceforth, Zerrbilder).

266. Ministry of the Interior, Deutsche Islam Konferenz, Auswahl von Empfehlungen und Schlussfolgerungen zu praxisrelevanten Themen (2006–2013), www.deutsche-islam-konferenz.de; DIK, faq-dokument. httpwww.deutsche-islam-konferenz.de

267. http://www.verfassungsschutz.de/, electronically accessed 05 Nov.2014, 04.22 IST.

268. Bundesamt fuer Migration und Fluechtlinge, Fragen und Antworten zur DIK in der zweiten Phase, www.deutsche-islam-konferenz.de, 17.05.2010, pp.2-3/7 (henceforth, Fragen und Antworten).

269. Oezdemir-Beck_Islamische-Verbaende-und-Religionsgemeinschaft.pdf

270. ECKHARD JESSE..., op.cit., p.1;. Fragen und Antworten, op.cit.

271. The ZDF forum was initially named differently but later changed to its present name. Www. Zeit.de, electronically accessed on 8 Januaray 2016, 7.53 pm IST; "Woher der Hass der Terroristen? Fragen an einen LKA-Mann", Forum am Freitag, www.zdf.de, 20 November 2015. Abdul Ahmad-Rashid's interview of a security expert. Electronically accessed on 11 January 2016, 8.15 pm IST.

272. Www.theguardian.com/world/charlie-hebdo-attack, 21 January 2016, 8.26 pm IST.

273. "Al-Azhar top cleric calls for religious teaching reform", http://www.bbc.com/news/world-middle-east-31580130, 23 February 2015. Electronically accessed on 24 April 2016, 1045 am IST. Ahmad Mansour is author of Generation Allah, a book critical of Salafism.

274. Samiha Shafy and Bernhard Zand , Saudi Foreign Minister: 'I Don't Think World War III Is Going To Happen in Syria'", http://www.spiegel.de/international/world/interview-with-saudi-foreign-minister-adel-al-jubeir-on-syrian-war-a-1078337.html, February 19, 2016 06:32 PM CET.
275. "'Time of looking away over': Germany warns Saudi Arabia to stop funding radical Islamists", https://www.rt.com/news/324936-germany-criticizes-saudi-arabia/,7 Dec, 2015 01:58 CET.
276. Kerstin Buecker, "Jetzt sind erst mal andere Staaten dran", http://www.bmi.bund.de/SharedDocs/Interviews/DE/2014/11/interview-kna.html, interview of de Maiziere on 28.11.2014. Electronically accessed on 24 April 2016, 8.31 pm IST.
277. In Greek mythology Daedalus, the inventor, created the labyrinth in Crete from which the uncouth Minotaur, a creature with a human body and a bull's head, could not escape. Theseus, a prince of Athens, on the other hand, managed to escape the labyrinth. Http://www.britannica.com/topic/Daedalus-Greek-mythology. Electronically accessed on 25 April 2016, 6.00 am IST.
278. James McAuley, "Two more suspects charged in investigation of Brussels attacks", https://www.washingtonpost.com/world/two-more-suspects-charged-in-brussels-attack-probe/2016/04/12/5e9e3866-c8a8-4f75-bdad-cc1e4c1f4ef1_story.html. Electronically accessed on 05 July 2016, 8.11 pm IST.
279. Quoting Pinak Ranjan Chakravarty, a former Indian diplomat and policy expert on Bangladesh, Katy Daigle, "Educated and well-off, Dhaka attackers defy usual', http://bigstory.ap.org/article/47b86f655ddc44129dc83f8317df64d0/educated-and-well-dhaka-attackers-defy-usual-profile, July 4, 2016 7:44 PM EDT.
280. The Telegraph, 29 July 2016, op. cit.
281. This investigative template consists of 8 proximal warning behaviors and 10 distal characteristics for active risk management or active monitoring, respectively, by national security threat assessors. Meloy, J. Reid; Gill, Paul, "The lone-actor terrorist and the TRAP-18", Journal of Threat Assessment and Management, Vol 3(1), Mar 2016, 37-52. http://dx.doi.org/10.1037/tam0000061, http://psycnet.apa.org/journals/tam/3/1/37/. Electronically accessed on 20 July 2016, 10.10 pm IST. See also Parvin Sadigh,"Terror oder Amok?"http://www.zeit.de/gesellschaft/zeitgeschehen/2016-07/attentaeter-amok-terror-attentate-nizza-orlando. Electronically accessed on 20 July 2016, 9.30 pm IST.
282. Sonia Sarkar, "Who's that Man?" The Telegraph, Kolkata, 10 July 2016, p. 11.
283. The Telegraph, Kolkata, 11 July 2016, p. 1.
284. Federal Ministry of the Interior 2014 ANNUAL REPORT…, op.cit, p.21.
285. Pitrim Sorokin, The American Sex Revolution (Boston: Porter Sargent, 1956); Herbert Marcuse, One-Dimensional Man (Boston: Beacon, 1964). Sorokin classified societies according to their 'cultural mentality', which can be "ideational" (reality is spiritual), "sensate" (reality

is material), or "idealistic" (a synthesis of the two). He offers three explanations for socio-cultural change: 1. external factors, 2, internal, immanent factors, 3. (Sorokin supports this) a combination of the two. Pitrim Sorokin, Social and Cultural Dynamics, revised and abridged in one volume by author, Porter Sargent Publisher, Boston, 1957, 2nd. printing 1970, pp.630-634, http://www.cfeps.org/ss2006/readings/Green-b.pdf, https://en.wikipedia.org/wiki/Pitirim_Sorokin; Alvin Toffler, Future Shock, Pan books Ltd, London, 1971, Chapters 15, 16, pp.296-333. Oswald Spengler's Decline of the West (Der Untergang des Abendlandes) presents a morphology of history and civilisations. It uses the terms of Apollonian/Magian/Faustian. These are Spengler's terms for Classical, Arabian and Western Cultures respectively. Apollonian Culture and Civilization is focused around Ancient Greece and Rome, the Magian relates to Muslims, Jews and Christians, as well as their Persian and Semitic forebears, and the Faustian Culture refers to the modern Westerner. The civilization of the West since the late nineteenth century, in Spengler's view, was exhibiting the same symptoms as ancient civilization in its decline. In the Magian world the separation of politics and religion is theoretically impossible and nonsensical, whereas in the Faustian Culture the battle of Church and State is inherent in the very conceptions logical, necessary, unending. In the Magian, civil and ecclesiastical law are simply identical. According to Spengler writing in the early 1920's, the Western world was ending, it was already in its last season"winter time"of Faustian Civilization. In Spengler's depiction, Western Man is a proud but tragic figure because, while he strives and creates, he secretly knows the actual goal will never be reached. Spengler vol II p.235, Spengler vol II p.243, http://spenglercrashcourse.blogspot.in/2009/12/problems-of-arabian-culture-b-magian.html, http://spenglercrashcourse.blogspot.in/2009/12/problems-of-arabian-culture-b-magian.html; https://en.wikipedia.org/wiki/The_Decline_of_the_West

286. See Radioeins (Berlin) interview of Ahmad Mansour, Israel-born psychologist living in Germany and working to prevent radicalisation. Gehört der Islam zu Deutschland? Working with youths, he says he noticed that they are looking for a definite road map of life. There is often a spiritual vacuum which only a bold ideology (or religion) can fill in. Http://www.radioeins.de/programm/index.htm/psdoc=%21content%21rbb%21rad%21programm%21sendungen%21sendungen%2199%211606%21160418_eins_sondersendung_25001.html. 27 June 2016, 8 pm CET.

287. Samuel P. Huntington, "The Clash of Civilizations?" Foreign Affairs, New York, Summer 1993 Issue, https://www.foreignaffairs.com/articles/united-states/1993-06-01/clash-civilizations. Electronically accessed on 26 July 2016, 9.10 pm IST. The essay later formed the basis of the book by the same title.

288. The Ramayana is an Indian epic in which Ramachandra, the princely hero of Ayodhya in exile, defeats the formidable king of Sri Lanka, Ravana, with the insidious help of the latter's brother, Bivishana.

289. See Leiken,op.cit.; Soeren Kern, "European Jihadists: The Latest Export", http://www.gatestoneinstitute.org/3634/european-jihadists, March 21, 2013 at 5:00 am ET; both Simpson and his room-mate companion were killed. Catherine Shoichet and Michael Pearson, "Garland, Texas, shooting suspect linked himself to ISIS in tweets",CNN, http://edition.cnn.com/2015/05/04/us/garland-mohammed-drawing-contest-shooting/, May 5, 201502.55 GMT.

290. Amartya Sen, The Argumentative Indian. Writings on Indian Culture, History and Identity, Penguin, London, 2005, pp.112-117. Sen cites Tagore in support of mass literacy.